BAKING TARTS FOR ALL OCCASIONS

FOR JACK AND CHARLIE, FOREVER MISSED.

BAKING TARTS FOR ALL OCCASIONS

DEBBY DONNELLY-ADDISON

WHITE OWL
AN IMPRINT OF PEN & SWORD BOOKS LTD.
YORKSHIRE – PHILADELPHIA

First published in Great Britain in 2026 by
White Owl
An imprint of
Pen & Sword Books Ltd
Yorkshire - Philadelphia

Print ISBN: 978 1 03614 287 2
ePUB ISBN: 978 1 03614 289 6
ePDF ISBN: 978 1 03614 291 9

A CIP catalogue record for this book is available from the British Library.

Typeset in 9/14 pts Open Sans
by SJmagic DESIGN SERVICES, India.
Printed and bound in India by Replika Press Pvt. Ltd

The Publisher's authorised representative in the EU for product safety is Authorised Rep Compliance Ltd., Ground Floor, 71 Lower Baggot Street, Dublin D02 P593, Ireland. www.arccompliance.com

For a complete list of Pen & Sword titles please contact

PEN & SWORD BOOKS LIMITED
George House, Beevor Street, Off Pontefract Road, Hoyle Mill, Barnsley,
South Yorkshire, England, S71 1HN.
E-mail: enquiries@pen-and-sword.co.uk
Website: www.pen-and-sword.co.uk

or

PEN AND SWORD BOOKS
1950 Lawrence Rd, Havertown, PA 19083, USA
E-mail: Uspen-and-sword@casematepublishers.com
Website: www.penandswordbooks.com

FSC
www.fsc.org
MIX
Paper | Supporting responsible forestry
FSC™ C016779

Contents

The Fillings

The Designs

Quick and Easy Decoration Ideas

Special Projects: Minis, Celebrations and More

Templates

Introduction

Well, hey there, friend! Thank you for buying this book. In just a few pages' time, you're going to be knee-deep in buttery, tarty goodness. But before we dive headfirst into this new adventure together, I wanted to take a moment to explain why I wrote this delicious little book, how this came to be, and how I hope it can become your companion in the kitchen.

Some of the designs or techniques you'll see might look a bit finicky at first glance, but don't worry, I've got your back. This isn't about achieving perfection. It's about creating something you can be proud of, something that smells divine, tastes divine and is utterly satisfying to serve (or to eat straight from the tin when nobody's looking).

I have been baking and sugar crafting since opening my shop, Vanilla Nova Cake Boutique, in 2010. These days, my kitchen is filled with every fancy tool imaginable: specialised tins, silicone mats, niche piping equipment that I've barely touched since purchase (I'm a sucker for a new gadget, it seems). For the most part, they've been essential to churn out thousands of wedding and celebration cakes over the past 16 years. But in the beginning, almost everything came from my home kitchen: forks for crimping pastry edges, pizza cutters for trimming icing, cocktail sticks for shaping sugar flowers – you name it, I probably improvised it. And you know what? I still use many of those same tools today.

That's the mindset I've kept while writing this book. With the exception of a few cheap moulds, I've tried to keep the equipment to things that you most likely have in your kitchen already: accessible, easy to use and realistic. There's the occasional ingredient you might need to buy in, but otherwise everything can be found in your local corner shop (if it is not in your pantry already). And the best part? I've used the same 20cm (8in) tart or flan tin for most of the recipes (special projects excluded). One tin. That's it. No faffing about with multiple sizes or quantities, no splashing out on a stack of bakeware. The majority of this book revolves around this single, trusty tin. Everything is built around that one piece of equipment, so you don't have to blow the kids' college fund on a multitude of tart tins.

Now, I know some of you may have skipped ahead to the pretty tart designs in the latter part of the book and are thinking: 'Deb, why can't I just buy a supermarket tart and decorate it?' Well, friend, guess what? You absolutely can. There is nothing wrong with only doing the bits you enjoy. If you just want a quick, delicious dessert without fussing over the pastry, that's perfectly fine. If store-bought pastry is your friend, use it. This book is meant to be joyful, not stressful. Stick to the parts that bring you joy and leave the rest behind.

Thanks to baking shows and social media, we've quietly accepted that baking is a complex science, a high-stakes performance that must be executed flawlessly. But it isn't. Yes, there is methodology, and yes, there are techniques, but there should never be shame in things not going according to plan. I bake for a living, and let me tell you, I've had bread collapse mid-bake, icing split, and yes, I've even thrown a wedding cake at a wall in sheer frustration. Some days just aren't your day, and that is fine.

When you bought this book, you also bought my silence. Decorate that store-bought cheesecake if you like, or make a bowl of tart filling and eat it under a blanket while binge-watching crime documentaries. I won't tell a soul. I've crammed these pages with hints and tips: from getting the best out of each recipe to advice for when things go a bit iffy. Trust me, these recipes rarely go wrong, but life happens: a knock at the door could mean a burnt custard, a heatwave could leave your sugar paste dry and unusable. I've sprinkled guidance notes throughout to help you out of any jam and give you the confidence to have another crack at it, even if the cat stepped on the last one.

A little bit about me: I started baking at university when a cake baked with £3 of ingredients (yes, I'm *that* old) was a much more cost-effective birthday gift from someone surviving on student loans. Soon, it was an escape, a way to focus on something joyous instead of the things that troubled me. In 2010, I fell very ill with a bone marrow condition and could no longer continue my career in law. Stuck between a rock and a hard place, I relied on cakes to pay the mortgage. For months, I was one Battenberg away from living in a skip, but then I took the leap and used my last £400 to open Vanilla Nova Cake Boutique. I've learned a lot on the job: what works, what doesn't, and how to fix things when they go sideways. I've learned to be creative, to work quietly and patiently, and to embrace the peace that baking can provide when the world feels too loud.

I chose to write about tarts because they are quick, versatile, and there's much less science involved than cakes (or the dreaded bread). Unlike cakes, which require rolled icing and delicate construction, tarts are flat, forgiving, and allow you to experiment with colours, fruits, flowers, creams and unusual ingredients without being intimidating. They're fun to play with, and there's room for mistakes, yet, with a bit of care, the results are wonderful. A delicious blank canvas on which to let your imagination run riot.

I hope this book becomes your space to slow down, experiment and enjoy. Whether you involve your children, a friend or just yourself, take pleasure in the process. The scent of buttery pastry turning golden in the oven, the creamy, silken texture of a well-made filling, the tiny rush of joy when you place the final flower petal *in situ*: these are the moments that make baking and sugar craft so deeply satisfying.

These recipes aren't complex. Some don't even require an oven. For those that do, all temperature settings are given in centigrade. Work your way through this book, at your own pace, enjoy the play, the mess and the unexpected successes. And, of course, share your creations, I would love to see them! Tag me on Instagram @thebohobaker and show me your tart art.

At the end of the day, this is about more than recipes. It's about carving out a little corner of calm in your day, creating something tangible and taking joy in the small, buttery, delicious victories. Welcome to the world of tarts. I'm so glad you're here.

Getting Started

TOOLS AND EQUIPMENT

- When it comes to tools and equipment, I like to keep things very simple. You don't need a whole arsenal of gadgets to make beautiful tarts; in fact, less is often more. A pizza cutter for cutting fondant, a sturdy wire rack for cooling and a good set of quality paintbrushes are my only essentials. Fine brushes, in particular, are worth spending a couple of extra pounds on to ensure you never find a rogue hair on your meticulously decorated creation. Most of the detailing in this book, whether background or intricate, is done using a large, fluffy dusting brush or an exceptionally fine one. Nothing in between usually gets an airing, so don't be conned into spending megabucks on a set that will never see the light of day. •
- If you've the space, curate a spare drawer of tools that might come in handy. You'd be amazed at how many ordinary household or craft items work brilliantly with sugar craft. For example, I often raid my (OK, my mum's) haberdashery stash: a fabric tracing wheel, normally used for marking patterns onto cloth, is perfect for tracing templates onto pastry. I also keep small cutters and needles designed for carving clay, as they're excellent for fine details and can make a world of difference when decorating. A clean sheet of muslin is excellent for creating a fabric effect on icing, just press and go. It's all about thinking creatively and seeing potential in everyday items.
- When it comes to your tart tin, you don't need to splash out. I've used the same Tala tin for the past 25 years, and it's still going strong. Try not to get too hung up on deciding between a solid base or a perforated one: as someone who has baked countless tarts, I can't say there is much merit in using one over the other. The only important thing is that it has a removable base. Without that, removing the tart can be a real headache, and you'll be tempted to frisbee it through the window. My trick? Simply slide a knife beneath the seams underneath the tin in case any sugar has hardened it into place, then pop it on top of a food tin or jam jar and ease the sides down gently. It works like a charm every time.

- Keeping your tools clean is paramount. If you're using metal implements, make sure they aren't blunted. If you're working with brushes, check that the ends haven't splayed. A lot of people make the mistake of washing brushes and leaving them to dry flat or upside down; this ruins the bristles and can leave you with unexpected splashes or uneven paint where you least want it. Snipping off any rogue bristles can help, but prevention is better than cure. Always leave your brushes to dry brush end up, in a tumbler, before packing them away.
- For melting chocolate, particularly for ganache recipes, I highly recommend investing in a small double boiler. These clever little pans hook on top of a saucepan, leaving your chocolate to melt gently over simmering water. Wilton makes an excellent one for under £10. The chocolate melts beautifully, and you avoid scorching it.
- Most of the extra items you'll see in these recipes – rice paper, spring roll wrappers (rice paper circles), edible colours – are easy to find in supermarkets, craft stores or online. I use a lot of rejuvenator spirit for painted details, but you can substitute any clear alcohol, such as vodka or gin. If you're baking with children, stick to rejuvenator spirit for safety.

A NOTE ON EDIBLE FLOWERS

Edible flowers are another area where care is important. Always source flowers that haven't been treated with chemicals or pesticides, and avoid plants from roadsides, garden centres or anywhere you can't guarantee purity. Nothing ruins a beautiful dessert quite like pesticides, or the odour of flowers that have been picked on a dog-walking route. If you can't guarantee provenance, don't put it on your bake: you could make yourself and your loved ones very poorly. The only safe edible flowers are those you have grown yourself (and are chemical-free), or those purchased from specialist ingredient websites. Some of the more upmarket supermarkets sell little tubs of edible violas during the summer months, perfect for adding a pop of colour safely.

A FEW HANDY TIPS AND TECHNIQUES I SWEAR BY

- **Arm support:** When painting or placing delicate decorations, rest your working arm on a rolled-up towel or your other forearm. This keeps things steady, prevents wobbles and helps avoid accidental smudges.

- **Tweezers:** Culinary tweezers are brilliant for placing small details, but any long-nosed, clean pair will do. They're especially helpful if your hands are shaky or if you're worried about misplacing tiny decorations on wet icing.
- **Glue:** I rarely buy edible glue. A tiny dab of water is usually enough to stick sugar to sugar. For rice paper, mix a few offcuts with water to make a sturdier paste. Flat tarts are forgiving, so a light touch is often all you need.
- **Stencil cutting:** Run a knife or small wheel around the stencil first, then remove it carefully and cut out the piece underneath. Don't try to cut through everything in one go: you'll save yourself a lot of frustration.
- **Edible colours:** Dusts and gels last much longer and have better vibrancy than watery supermarket varieties. There's very little difference in terms of cost, and you don't need to use as much product.

And finally, remember to keep your sense of humour. Things will go wrong. Things will go right. You might spill, smudge or misplace a decoration. Your sugar bunny might be cross-eyed, your fondant bees may look like hornets, it's all part of the dance. Baking is as much about the journey as the finished tart. Enjoy the process. Laugh at the mishaps. Celebrate the successes. The tools and techniques are just guides – your creativity, patience and joy are what truly make these tarts memorable.

INGREDIENTS AND PANTRY ESSENTIALS

When it comes to baking anything, the first thing you'll realise is that the ingredients themselves are your real heroes. You can have the fanciest decoration techniques and the most elaborate designs, but if the base ingredients aren't up to scratch, the whole thing can fall a little flat (dry cake, anyone?). Luckily, most of what you need is simple, accessible and, in many cases, you might already have it lurking in your kitchen cupboards. Let's talk about the ingredients that will make your tarts sing, as well as a few pantry hacks to make your baking smoother, tastier and a lot more fun.

Butter

Butter is, without a doubt, the backbone of any tart pastry. It's rich, it's flavourful and it gives your crust that tender, melt-in-the-mouth quality we all hope to achieve. Any good-quality unsalted butter will work in these recipes: the brand and supermarket of origin does not make a jot of difference if it is pure butter. There are hybrid spreads and bottled butter products that can be poured, but the results in terms of both taste and texture will not be the same. I personally always choose unsalted because it lets me control the level of salt, particularly in sweet pastry cases. You never know how much salt is in a block of salted butter, so it can be difficult to balance other salty ingredients such as nuts and salted caramel.

When working with butter, temperature is everything. Too soft, and your pastry will slump; too hard, and it won't blend properly with the flour. I often keep my butter in small cubes in the fridge, ready to toss straight into the flour. If your kitchen is warm, a quick 10–15 minutes in the fridge will firm it back up before you start rolling. Alternatively, toss the butter in the flour and place the bowl containing both ingredients in the freezer for 5 minutes before rubbing it all together.

And a little tip that's saved me countless times: if you feel the butter 'coming through' your pastry when rolling it out, wrap your pastry in clingfilm, flatten it into a disc and pop it back in the fridge. Patience here is key: for the sake of an extra 10 minutes in the fridge, you will be rewarded with beautifully flaky pastry post-bake.

Flour

Plain flour, almond flour, self-raising flour, so many varieties, each with their own role. Plain flour is the most versatile and what you'll use in almost all the classic tart bases. We don't use self-raising flour here because, well, we don't want our bases to rise. We want a crisp, flaky pastry, free from bubbles. I also adore incorporating nut flours, like almond or pistachio, especially when making frangipane tarts. Nut flours bring a subtle richness and texture that you cannot achieve with regular flour, plus many are gluten-free (although you should always check the packaging before use).

It is crucial that you measure flour carefully. Spoon it lightly into the cup or weigh it on a scale. Scooping straight from the bag can pack it down and leave you with a pastry that's dry and crumbly. Precision matters, but not so much that it becomes stressful. Give the spoon a little jiggle from side to side as you transfer the flour to your bowl, or even better, pass it through a sieve before adding the butter.

Finally, remember to dust your worktop *lightly* when kneading/rolling out pastry. A heavy dusting could result in an extra 10g of flour added to your recipe, compromising the end result.

Sugar

Sugar isn't just about sweetness; it affects texture, colour, and even the way your pastry holds together. There's caster sugar, icing sugar, muscovado, light brown, dark brown, the list goes on. Ideally, you need to be using caster sugar for pastries and light brown sugar for fillings like caramel or frangipane. Muscovado has a lovely depth and works beautifully in winter-spiced tarts.

Sugar also plays a huge role in toppings and decorations. A sprinkling of icing sugar over a tart can cover a multitude of sins, whereas a dusting of cocoa, or a light sprinkle of coarse sugar for crunch, can completely change the final presentation. And don't forget, when you're using sugar for brushing edges or creating a snow effect, a light hand goes a long way.

Eggs

Eggs are the unsung heroes of any bake: they bind, enrich, and even give a golden sheen to baked cases. I like to use medium or large free-range eggs, always at room temperature (if you keep yours in the fridge, leave them out for 15 minutes to warm up a little before use). Cold eggs can 'shock' the butter and flour mixture, making your pastry less pliable.

Eggs are also crucial in custards, frangipanes and other baked fillings. When whisking egg yolks for a custard, always combine with sugar first and allow your pan of liquid to cool for at least 2 minutes before mixing to ensure they don't scramble. A little care goes a long way, and it's these small details that separate a good tart from a great one.

Dairy

Double cream, single cream, milk and, occasionally, crème fraîche or mascarpone, dairy provides the richness and mouthfeel. Double cream is essential in most of my tarts for fillings, ganaches and toppings. Whip it gently to soft peaks, fold into cream cheese or mascarpone mixtures, and suddenly your tart is elevated to something silken and luxurious. No oven required.

A handy trick: if your cream splits or isn't holding, place the bowl over a pan of warm water and whisk gently. It's amazing how forgiving cream can be when treated with a little care.

Milk is mostly used for custards or light fillings. Whole milk gives the best flavour and body, but you are welcome to adapt these recipes and use plant-based alternatives if you prefer dairy-free options. Almond milk, oat milk and coconut milk can all work, but adjust sweetness and richness accordingly.

Chocolate

Chocolate is a wonderful ingredient for both fillings and decoration. When working with chocolate, I strongly recommend using a double boiler or a melting pan that floats on top of a simmering saucepan. This prevents scorching and helps achieve that silky texture every tart deserves.

I keep chocolate at room temperature in a cool, dry cupboard and always break it into even pieces for melting. It helps it melt evenly, whether it's for ganache, drizzling or a chocolate tart base. As for quality, aim for at least 70% cocoa content for your dark chocolate: it won't be bitter once it is mixed with cream or other ingredients. Anything less will become diluted by the dairy components, and the richness will be lost (which is why I don't use milk chocolate in any of my recipes). When it comes to white chocolate, anything goes. In fact, I use the cheapest supermarket own-brand I can get my hands on. Unless you are eating it straight from the bar, there is very little taste difference when using it as an ingredient.

Nuts and Seeds

Nuts can provide texture, flavour and structure. Toasting them lightly brings out their natural oils and adds a deep, nutty aroma. Ground nuts can be used in tart bases or fillings, while chopped nuts make a lovely finishing touch. Nut flours, such as almond and hazelnut, are excellent gluten-free options if you cannot consume regular flour, but please check the packaging to ensure purity and safety before using.

If you're adding nuts to a pastry case, make sure they're evenly distributed so the tart bakes consistently (nobody wants to find a clump in their flaky pastry base). Seeds like pumpkin or sesame can also add crunch and a subtle layer of complexity. I always keep a small stash of both toasted and raw nuts on hand: it's amazing how much they can elevate any bake.

Fruit and Herbs

Fruit is an absolute godsend for decorating in a hurry or when you're not feeling particularly artistic. Just chop 'em up and throw 'em on. Seasonal fruits are particularly good, as they're at their peak flavour and colour. Berries in summer, apples and pears in autumn, citrus in winter – matching fruit to season is an easy way to get vibrant results without forcing ingredients out of season. If you can, add some fresh herbs (such as mint, rosemary or thyme) and a dusting of icing sugar for whimsy.

For tinned or preserved fruits, always drain excess liquid to prevent sogginess. A quick tip: macerating fresh berries with a touch of sugar and lemon juice intensifies flavour and adds a lovely shine when decorating.

Spices and Flavourings

Vanilla, cinnamon, nutmeg, cardamom, star anise, zest from lemons and limes: these are the magical finishing flourishes. Even a small pinch can completely transform a filling. I encourage experimentation, especially when pairing spices with seasonal fruits. Vanilla is my default for creams and custards, but a hint of cardamom or sprig of thyme will elevate your dessert to another level. Nutmeg will provide depth, while cinnamon gives a comforting edge. Play about, just keep cloves out of it.

Zests are another way to add freshness without extra sugar. Always zest lightly and avoid the bitter white pith underneath the skin.

Cereals and Other Silliness

I like to keep a variety of long-life products to hand so I have ingredients to experiment with when I'm feeling creative: puffed rice cereal, jellybeans, biscotti, macaroons, jars of marshmallow fluff, assorted chocolate, speculoos (cookie butter) spreads and unfamiliar biscuits from other parts of the world. It's good to have a stash of random bits to play with, especially when baking with children. Have a play and see what you can come up with.

Extras and Pantry Hacks

Some extra items might not seem essential, but they can make your life so much easier.

- **Rice paper:** An incredibly versatile addition that can be used to make edible glue, fluffy decorations, edible lace and tulle.
- **Spring-roll wrappers:** Brilliant for ethereal 'sail' decorations (you can find the guide for this later in this book).
- **Edible colours:** Dusts and gels work better than watery supermarket varieties, which are often a false economy and have poor vibrancy. Brands such as Sugarflair and Rainbow Dust are readily available online and will last a couple of years.
- **Culinary/long nosed tweezers:** Invaluable for placing tiny decorations.
- **Rejuvenator spirits or clear alcohol:** For painting decorations. A small amount mixed with edible dust colours will go a long, long way.

Storage Tips

A well-stocked and organised pantry is a baker's best friend. Even if your 'baking pantry' comprises of one shelf in a small cupboard, treating your ingredients right will make them last longer, taste better and, well, free of critters who would love nothing more than to bathe in a bag of sugar.

- Keep flours, sugars, and nuts in airtight containers to maintain freshness.
- Chocolate prefers a cool, dry, dark place: never the fridge.
- Store spices in small jars, away from light and heat.
- Eggs should always be at room temperature, even if you store them in the fridge between baking sessions.
- Butter should be refrigerated and only brought out of the fridge beforehand if the recipe calls for the butter to be softened.
- Bicarbonate of soda and baking powder lose efficacy rather quickly. Even if you have stored it well, don't be tempted to dig out the tub from two Christmases ago. If it hasn't been used in 12 months, replace it with a fresh tub.

Inspiration and Experimentation

Finally, a few thoughts to inspire creativity.

- Mix and match flavours: chocolate with orange, pistachio with rose, caramel with sea salt. I have added pairing suggestions with each recipe, but my recommendations are by no means exhaustive. Have a play around and see what gets you excited.
- Don't be afraid to adapt fillings to what you have on hand. Not enough ingredients for a full tart's worth of ganache? Add a layer of marmalade underneath to bulk it out and create a new flavour combination. Want something with a bit more zing? Mix whole berries in with your cream cheese filling. There are countless options to zhush up your dessert if you're brave enough to try something different.
- Encourage family and friends to taste-test your experiments: they might suggest flavour combinations you hadn't considered! Although you might want to ignore your pregnant cousin's pickle and cream cheese idea ...

Remember, your pantry is more than a storage space. It's a playground. With a few staples, a bit of seasonal inspiration and your creativity, you can make hundreds of variations on these tarts.

INGREDIENT TECHNIQUES AND TRICKS

When it comes to baking, the ingredients themselves are the basic building materials: knowing how to handle them is what separates a good tart from a spectacular one. I've picked up plenty of little tricks, cheats and techniques that make baking smoother, easier and just more fun. Some of these might seem obvious, some a little quirky, but they save a *lot* of time and stress in the kitchen.

Butter and Pastry

- **Cubing and chilling:** Always cut butter into small cubes before adding it to flour. This ensures even distribution and makes it easier to rub it in, creating that breadcrumb texture that leads to perfect pastry. If the kitchen is warm, refrigerate for 10–15 minutes before chopping.
- **Softening tricks:** Need butter soft quickly? Use a cheese grater to grate it directly into the flour. Alternatively, fill a glass jug with boiling water and let it sit for 30 seconds. Tip the water out, then place the empty jug over the butter. The residual heat will soften the butter without the harshness of a microwave or hob.
- **Pro pastry:** If you're serious about perfect pastry, cube the butter, toss it in the flour, and place the bowl containing both ingredients in the freezer for 15 minutes before rubbing it together. Use iced water as your binding agent for extra flakiness.
- **Rolling out pastry:** Lightly flour your surface and rolling pin, but not so much that it dries the pastry. Roll gently from the centre outward, turning frequently to maintain an even circle. If your kitchen is humid, you can roll the pastry between two sheets of greaseproof paper to keep it from sticking to the pin or worktop.

Flour and Dry Ingredients

- **Unpacking:** Sieve flour into the bowl rather than scooping directly from the bag. Packed flour = dense pastry. If you don't have a sieve, at least give the spoon a little jiggle to prevent clumping.
- **Precision:** If you can, always use a digital scale. If using volume (cup) measurements, don't pack your ingredients down.
- **Sifting:** Sifting can aerate flours, cocoa and powdered sugar, giving your tarts a lighter, more delicate texture. For a super-fine texture with nut flours/ground almonds, sieve three times. Yes, it's a faff, but the difference in texture post-bake is remarkable.

Eggs

- **Room temperature:** I store my eggs at room temperature, but if you keep yours in the fridge, please bring them out at least 15 minutes before use. Cold eggs can shock butter and cream mixtures, creating lumps or preventing proper aeration.
- **Whisking techniques:** When making custards, always mix eggs with sugar first. This helps them emulsify properly when hot liquids are added. Leave the cream and milk mixture to cool for a couple of minutes before pouring, then whisk in slowly to prevent scrambling.
- **Ensuring freshness:** If your eggs are not dated and you are unsure of their freshness, carefully place them in a large bowl or jug filled with water. If the egg stands upright or floats, it is past its best and should not be consumed.

Cream and Dairy

- **Whipping/double cream:** Most fillings require whipping/double cream whipped to soft peaks. This means the cream holds shape but is still slightly soft, perfect for folding into mousses and custards. Overwhipping can create a grainy texture so remember, we're not talking about those meringue videos you've seen where you can hold the bowl upside down and nothing budges. The cream should be soft, silky, with a little structure, but not firm.
- **Single cream:** Does not belong here! It doesn't have the body and oomph needed for whipping so please stick to thicker, sturdier products.
- **Stabilising cream:** If your cream splits or becomes too soft, place the bowl over a pan of gently simmering water and whisk lightly: it will magically come back together.
- **Substitutions:** Plant-based creams can work, but reduce liquid elsewhere in the recipe and be mindful of sweetness (taste and adjust as you go). Thick coconut cream is an excellent alternative but requires a little more whipping. If you're struggling to get it to stabilise, add a spoonful of caster sugar and try again.

Chocolate

- **Melting:** Use a double boiler or a chocolate melting pan that sits over simmering water. This prevents scorching and keeps chocolate glossy.
- **Chopping evenly:** Always chop chocolate into similar-sized pieces. Smaller pieces melt more evenly and reduce the risk of burning.
- **Cooling:** Allow melted chocolate to cool slightly before adding eggs or cream to prevent curdling.

- **Clumping:** If your chocolate seems a little thick, add a dash of vegetable or sunflower oil and return to a gentle heat. If your chocolate has seized completely, it can sometimes be rescued with a little extra cream, milk or butter; just heat and mix. However, please note that you won't achieve the 'snap' texture once extra ingredients have been added, so this is only good for ganache and coating rather than edible decorations or chocolate bars.

Nuts

- **Toasting:** Lightly toast nuts in a dry pan for a few minutes. This brings out oils, aroma and flavour. Let them cool before chopping.
- **Grinding:** Use a food processor for fine nut flours. For a rustic texture, bash them gently in a bag with a rolling pin or use a pestle and mortar.
- **Even distribution:** Scatter nuts evenly across fillings or pastry cases to avoid dense clumps in one bite. Without meaning to sound too finicky, I like to scatter the nuts over the top and then use my tweezers to break up any crowded areas and create a slightly more polished result.

Fruit

- **Fresh:** Always wash, dry and hull fruits before adding to tarts. Berries benefit from a light maceration with sugar and a squeeze of lemon juice (or alcohol, if you're that way inclined). If you've picked fruit or berries yourself, leave the container out for an hour or two before using, to allow any hidden critters to escape.
- **Dried:** Chop dried fruits evenly; soak if needed to soften them.
- **Tinned:** Drain excess liquid thoroughly: soggy tarts are the worst. For a fruity bonus, reserve the liquid and heat it in a pan with a tablespoon of sugar and a dash of lemon juice or booze. Reduce by a third and use to glaze fruit or drizzle over your tart slices before serving.

Spices and Zests

- **Zesting citrus:** Avoid the bitter white pith. Zest in long, thin strips, or finely grate, for a delicate flavour. As tempting as it is to use the cheese grater for this, please don't: you need a super-fine grater, which can be picked up for a couple of pounds and can be used for many other things, such as nutmeg or grating chocolate over a hot cup of cocoa.
- **Spice blooming:** Toast ground spices lightly in a dry pan for 10–20 seconds to intensify aroma and have you house smelling like a fancy bakery.
- **Measuring small quantities:** A tiny pinch can go a long way: start small, taste, adjust.

Sugar

- **Texture and function:** Granulated sugar gives structure; caster sugar is best for smooth pastries; icing sugar adds a soft dusting. Please do not try to substitute one for the other: texture has a huge effect on the finished result. If you don't believe me, try adding a spoonful of icing sugar to your cup of tea and let me know how it tastes.
- **Caramelisation:** When making caramel, resist the urge to stir until the sugar melts. Swirl gently if needed, but do not stir or you risk the sugar crystallising. Add cream slowly and whisk constantly to avoid splitting.
- **Blitzing:** If you are absolutely stuck and need a quick solution, regular sugar can be blitzed in a processor to create icing sugar. However, it will need sifting several times to achieve the lightness of store-bought. You can use regular sugar in place of caster sugar if you must, but it won't be as light and airy as you would have liked.

General Tricks

- **Everything in place:** Prep everything before starting. Have butter cubed, eggs at room temperature, nuts chopped and fruits ready. Baking is smoother when nothing is last-minute, and having your ingredients set out in front of you will make you feel like a pro and give others the impression that you actually know what you're doing (which you do, of course).
- **Using tools wisely:** Even simple household items such as pizza cutters, forks and cookie cutters can double as pastry tools. Keep a 'bakers' drawer' for handy items.
- **Cleanliness and order:** Keep your workspace tidy. It saves stress and makes decorating far more enjoyable. I keep a pastry scraper and scraps bowl to hand so I can constantly scrape any worktop crumbs and excess into the bowl and out of my way. If you are spraying any cleaning solution between steps, be sure to wipe it down with clean water twice afterwards: you don't want to taint the pastry when rolling.

TROUBLESHOOTING AND COMMON MISTAKES

Even the best of us, the ones with perfectly sharpened tools and meticulously measured ingredients, run into issues from time to time. Don't panic. Baking is part science, part art and 100% patience. I've had plenty of disasters, and if you follow these tips you'll mostly avoid the same pitfalls. And if not? Laugh it off, taste it anyway and try again.

Pastry and Crusts

Shrinking Pastry

My heart sinks at the sight of shrunken pastry: there's nothing more frustrating than opening the oven door and finding your carefully-made pastry barely reaches the edges. This usually happens if the pastry was handled too much or was too warm when it hit the oven. Keep your ingredients cold, your hands gentle and don't panic if it shrinks a little: it tastes the same. If you have warm hands or simply cannot help handling the pastry too much (and it's an easy thing to do if you have arthritis or sore joints), then give your pastry case an extra-long stint in the fridge before baking. I'm talking 30–60 minutes here to allow the butter to solidify and the ingredients to settle. Preheat the oven 10 minutes before transferring the pastry case from the fridge and throw it right in.

Slumpy or Soggy Bases

This one's often caused by wet fillings or not blind baking. Always prick your base several times with a fork before baking, and, if required, bake with baking beans/uncooked rice for a short while first. For extra safety, brush the base lightly with melted chocolate and leave it to set before adding any super-soft fillings such as tinned fruit. It creates a moisture barrier and prevents a soggy foundation from developing.

Cracks in the Pastry

Too dry or rolled too thin? Don't worry. Patch with extra scraps of dough and press with a little warmth from your fingers. Imperfections don't ruin the taste, I promise.

If you consistently have issues with pastry tearing when lining the tin, use my cheat method of rolling the pastry into a log, slicing it into thin discs, and pressing them into the tart tin. Just make sure that no gaps are remaining and the sides are fully covered with a slight overhang.

Tough Pastry

Overworking is the culprit. Rub in the butter gently and only add water a little at a time. If your pastry has gone tough, it can still be used but it won't be as light as you might like. Serve it warm and slathered with hot custard; that tough base won't be an issue.

Uneven Baking

Ovens have moods (mine is permanently hot-headed and raging). 'Hot spots' do exist: you will most certainly have one part of your oven that is hotter than the rest, so get to know where that is. If your edges are browning too fast, a strip of foil around the perimeter can help, just remember to remove it 5 minutes before taking the tart out of the oven. Alternatively, rotate the tin every so often to ensure an even bake. Unlike cakes and bread, tarts don't rise, so releasing heat by opening the oven door isn't as disastrous as it would be for a batch of muffins.

Sticking to the Tin

Always use a tin with a removable base. If the tart sticks, place the tin on a jam jar or small can, push the sides down gently, and it should come free. If it doesn't, run a knife between the seam underneath the tart tin to loosen any hardened sugar that may be keeping them glued together.

Custards and Baked Fillings

Splitting or Curdling Custard

Eggs and heat don't always get along. Whisk slowly, temper your eggs by adding a little hot liquid before pouring it all in, and bake low and slow. If the mix does split and you catch it quickly, whisk it over a double boiler (a heatproof bowl set over a pan of barely simmering water) and it will come back together like magic. If it's too far gone, you've now got scrambled eggs for lunch.

Wobbly or Under-set Filling

This usually means it needs more time or a slightly higher oven temperature. Don't be afraid to leave it an extra 5–10 minutes: ovens can vary wildly when it comes to temperature, so get to know yours or, even better, buy an oven thermometer. The centre should wobble just slightly when done, setting to a jelly-like wibble by the time it has fully cooled. If it is wobbling all the way to the edges, pop it back in the oven for a little longer.

Over-baked or Rubbery Custard

Keep your eye on it! Set your timer and remember, the residual/internal heat keeps cooking after the tart has left the oven. Don't wait for the centre to be fully set before taking it out to cool.

Lumpy Custard

Strain your custard before pouring it into the tart case. Simple and an absolute game-changer. A fine mesh sieve will catch any bits of cooked egg, leaving you with a smooth, silky custard. If you don't have a sieve, a tea strainer or a piece of muslin will do. Old school cooks used a clean pair of tights, although you might not want to splash pictures of that method on Instagram.

Surface Cracks

Gentle heat and gradual cooling are key (which is why we never cool baked goods in the fridge. Room temperature only, please). If cracks appear, cover lightly with whipped cream or decorative fruit. Nobody will notice.

Chilled and Cream Fillings

Soft Whipped Cream/Cheeses Not Holding Shape

Keep your ingredients in the fridge up until the moment you use them, and don't overmix. Chill your bowl and beaters if you need to, and use balloon whisks if you have them (they generate more air than paddle beaters). Patience is the real secret ingredient.

Mousse Collapsing

Aerated desserts are delicate. Fold gently and chill immediately. If it sinks or collapses slightly, cover the offending parts with edible flowers or a stack of fresh berries.

Sugar or Flavouring Affecting Texture

Adding liquid extracts or alcohol? Use sparingly, and adjust other liquids accordingly. Too much and your filling can go soupy.

Meringue Not Coming Together

Meringues need time and patience. Add a spoonful of your sugar and whisk for a minute before adding the next, and so on. Ensure the bowl is scrupulously clean before starting, as any traces of oil can wreak havoc and prevent your meringue from coming together.

Chocolate and Caramel

Chocolate Seizing

Dry chocolate and water do not mix. Keep your bowls dry and melt your chocolate in a double boiler (a heatproof bowl over a pan of simmering water) if possible. Do not let the simmering water touch the base of the bowl, and keep the heat low to keep the steam from rising. Alternatively, you can melt the chocolate in short bursts in the microwave, but it's more liable to seize as you have less control over the heat. If it starts to look thick, add a spoonful of fat (butter, oil, milk or cream), and heat gently, whisking continuously.

Ganache Too Thick/Too Thin

Add a spoonful of double/whipping cream to loosen, or let it cool slightly to thicken. Depending on the room temperature and humidity, ganache can take some time to set. If it isn't showing any signs of firming up after two hours, pop it in the fridge.

Caramel Crystallising

Sugar crystals are sneaky little rascals that can ruin your hard work in a matter of seconds. When heating sugar for caramel, brush the pan edges with a wet pastry brush while melting. Sadly, if the sugar is looking dry and crunchy and won't melt back down, you need to start again.

Caramel Tart Too Runny

Cool the caramel slightly before adding to your tart, and don't pour the caramel into a fridge-cold crust straight from the stove. Give the caramel a minute to cool, and make sure the crust is at room temperature before pouring.

Fruit and Topping Issues

Soggy Fruit/Tart Base

Pat fruit dry and macerate lightly with sugar to draw out excess juice (this simply means tossing the fruit in sugar and leaving it to do its thing overnight). If it's a warm day or the tart is part of a spread at room temperature, try not to add the fruit until the last minute.

Fruit Browning

Use a light coating of jam, sugar syrup or lemon juice to preserve colour. If you are using tinned fruit, heat the juices with a tablespoon of sugar and dash of lemon juice. Reduce by a third and brush over the fruit before placing it on the tart.

Uneven Distribution of Toppings

Plan it out! Start from the centre or the edges, and place with tweezers if needed. If moving a piece of fruit or decoration leaves a mark underneath, you may be able to clean it up using a cotton bud or a damp paintbrush.

Decorations not Sticking

No fancy glue required here! A dab with a damp paintbrush is often enough. For heavier decorations like rice paper, create a slightly thicker glue by mixing the offcuts with water.

Decorative boo-boos

Painted Decorations Smudging

Work slowly and keep your brushes clean and upright when drying. Check for any rogue bristles, removing any jaunty ones before painting. Be careful not to add too much liquid to your paint to avoid spreading. And, finally, lean your arm on a towel or your other forearm to stabilise.

Edible Glue Failing

Use water for sugar-to-sugar sticking. For rice paper, thicker glue made from a few offcuts in water provides much more stability.

Flowers Wilting/Browning

Use only pesticide-free, edible flowers. Add them last, right before serving. If you are unsure whether a flower is safe to eat, do not put it on your tart.

Sugar Dusting Clumping

Use a fine sieve, and don't overload the tart. For icing sugar over cream, do it just before serving to keep it from clagging or looking patchy.

Colouring Uneven/Patchy

Dusts and gels yield the best results. If you get part way through decorating and are worried it's looking a bit too uneven, why not lean into it and go for a watercolour effect? Add dashes of other colours loosened with a few drops of rejuvenator spirit or clear alcohol. Finish with a few petals and it will no doubt look intentional.

The Crusts

I get it: it can be tempting to play safe and just stick to the refrigerated crusts, but trust me, their baked counterparts aren't as difficult as they appear. Baked cases are generally more stable, provide a thinner, crispier crust, and take less time to set. Plus, I'm going to teach you how to make them in the easiest way possible. Huzzah!

In this chapter, you will find a large variety of baked and refrigerated tart crusts. You can mix and match the fillings as you wish, although, being the Cilla Black of tarts that I am, I've added recommended pairings along the way.

COLD CRUSTS

Refrigerated crusts are an excellent option for baking with kids, or if you're just not fussed on working with heat. As long as you are mindful of crumb size (we will get to that in a second) and ensure the crust has ample time to chill, you really cannot go wrong. With the exception of the marshmallow cereal crust (which is far more pliable than the others), it is important that you break down the dry ingredient as much as possible. A quick blitz in a food processor is ideal, but if you don't have one to hand, tip the cereal/biscuits into a food-safe bag, cover with a tea towel and give it a ruddy good bash with a rolling pin.

You don't need to grease the tin before using: the crust will be firm enough to slide right out. If it feels a little stuck after chilling, just flip the tin over and run a knife through the seam beneath the base before placing the tin on top of a mug and sliding the tin away from the crust.

BAKED CRUSTS

There's the traditional way of lining a tart tin, or there's the cheat method. Fortunately for you, dear reader, I am going to teach you both.

The traditional method

- You want to handle your pastry as little as possible, so make sure you have everything out and ready in advance.
- Dust the worktop with as little flour as possible to ensure you are not adding to the pastry. Roll the dough out to approximately 5mm thick.
- You can transfer the dough to the tin by sliding a large pastry scraper underneath or placing your rolling pin on the edge of the pastry sheet, rolling the dough around the pin, and then unrolling it over the tart case.
- Leave a little pastry overhang when trimming away the excess. This will help accommodate any shrinkage that may occur while the tart is in the oven.
- Finish by baking as per the instructions of the recipe.

The Shortcut

If you're not into all that floury, roly-poly action, then fear not, for I have an alternative. Once the tart has been filled, the only visible difference can be seen from beneath the base. If your guests are the kind of people who flip their dessert over to check the integrity of the pastry, it's time to find better friends.

There are two ways you can go about lining your tin using this method:

- Roll the pastry into a cylinder and wrap tightly in cling film before refrigerating for at least 30 minutes. When you are ready to line the tart tin, unwrap the pastry and cut the cylinder into 5mm discs. Press the discs into the tart tin, ensuring all gaps are filled and all edges are sealed.
- The second method is particularly helpful if you have warm hands and struggle to keep pastry cool when handling. Dust the worktop with a little flour and roll the pastry into a sheet approximately 5mm thick. Using a cookie/scone cutter, cut the pastry into discs and use them to line your tart tin. Easy-peasy.

Crust Recipes

Almond

60 MINS BAKED

METHOD

1. Preheat the oven to 180°/160° (fan)/gas mark 4.
2. Combine the ground almonds and salt in a large bowl.
3. Melt the butter in short spurts in the microwave. Alternatively, you can melt it in a pan over a low heat on the hob, but do keep an eye on it to ensure it doesn't burn.
4. Pour the melted butter into the bowl of dry ingredients. Add the maple syrup and give the mixture a jolly good stir. Turn the dough out onto a sheet of cling film, wrap firmly, and refrigerate for 30 mins.
5. Turn the dough out onto a lightly floured worktop and roll to a thickness of about 5mm. Slide a large pastry lifter under the sheet of dough and transfer it to your tart tin. If you don't have a pastry lifter, slide a knife under the pastry sheet before you attempt to lift it to ensure it's not stuck to the worktop. If your pastry tears during the move, don't panic: you can patch it up, using the warmth of your hands to seal any torn edges. It will taste delicious nonetheless.
6. Trim the edges of the pastry to approximately 5mm over the top of the tart tin and pop it in the fridge for 10 mins.
7. Remove the tart case from the fridge and prick the base several times with a fork. Bake in the oven for 12 mins.
8. Upon removing the tart case from the oven, swiftly transfer the tin to a wire rack and trim the pastry edges with a sharp knife or scissors. Leave to cool in its tin before removing.

INGREDIENTS

250G GROUND ALMONDS

60G UNSALTED BUTTER

3 TBSP MAPLE SYRUP

½ TSP SALT

Candied Pecan

90 MINS CHILLED

INGREDIENTS

150G PECAN HALVES

100G CASTER SUGAR

1 TSP GROUND CINNAMON

½ TSP SALT

1 MEDIUM EGG WHITE

1 TSP WATER

40G BUTTER, MELTED

METHOD

1. Preheat the oven to 150°/130° (fan)/ gas mark 2. Line a baking tray with baking paper.
2. In a small bowl, whisk the egg white and water until frothy but not stiff.
3. In a separate bowl, mix the sugar, cinnamon and salt.
4. Add the pecans to the egg white mixture and stir until evenly coated. Tip the sugared spice mix over the pecans and stir again so every nut is covered in a grainy, sandy coating.
5. Spread the pecans out on the tray in a single layer and bake for 25–30 mins, giving them a stir halfway through. Leave to firm up as they cool.
6. Bash the candied pecans using a pestle and mortar or a rolling pin.
7. Add the melted butter, stirring until the pecans are well coated.
8. Transfer the mixture to the tart tin and press it into the base and sides. Refrigerate for 30 mins, or until firm.

Recommended fillings: maple pecan, mascarpone cream.

Bran Flake and Honey

10 MINS CHILLED

INGREDIENTS

200G BRAN FLAKES

80G HONEY

60G BUTTER

METHOD

1. Tip the bran flakes into a bowl and give them a light bash with the end of a rolling pin.
2. Melt the butter and honey together over a low heat. Pour the mixture into the bran flakes and stir until well combined.
3. Press the mixture into the tart tin and refrigerate for at least 30 mins, or until set.

Recommended fillings: lemon and lime, mascarpone cream.

Cheat's Carrot Cake

30 MINS BAKED

INGREDIENTS

200G STORE-BOUGHT CARROT CAKE

50G DIGESTIVE BISCUITS

50G BUTTER, MELTED

METHOD

1. Preheat the oven to 180°/160° (fan)/ gas mark 4.
2. Crumble the carrot cake into a bowl. Add the crushed digestives.
3. Stir in the melted butter before pressing the mixture into the tart tin.
4. Bake in the oven for 15 mins to firm back up. Leave to cool completely before removing from the tin.

Recommended fillings: carrot cake and cream cheese, mascarpone cream, anything with a bit of bite.

Marshmallow Cereal

2.5 HOURS

CHILLED

INGREDIENTS

70G PUFFED RICE CEREAL

100G MARSHMALLOWS

2 TBSP MILK

50G SMARTIES, CRUSHED

Tip: Try switching out the Smarties for freeze-dried strawberries or chopped dark chocolate.

METHOD

1. Combine the marshmallows and milk in a pan. Gently heat until the marshmallows are transformed into a gloriously silky, sticky mess.
2. Remove the pan from the heat and stir in the puffed rice cereal. Leave the mixture to cool for a minute before stirring in the Smarties.
3. Fill a deep bowl or pan with cold water. Spoon half of the marshmallow mixture into the tart tin. Dip your hands in the cold water and press the cereal into the grooves of the tin. Add the remaining mixture and work it into the tin, dipping your hands in the cold water as you go (this will prevent it from sticking to you). Refrigerate for at least 2 hours, preferably overnight, before filling.

Oat and Brown Sugar Crunch

40 MINS BAKED

INGREDIENTS

150G ROLLED OATS (PORRIDGE WILL DO)

80G PLAIN FLOUR

70G BROWN SUGAR

90G UNSALTED BUTTER, MELTED

Tip: This is an excellently crisp base for wet fillings as long as you really press it into the tart tin before baking.

METHOD

1. Preheat the oven to 180°/160° (fan)/gas mark 4.
2. Mix oats, flour and sugar in a bowl. Stir in melted butter until well combined.
3. Press into tart tin, ensuring even coverage. Prick the base several times with a fork and refrigerate for 20 mins.
4. Transfer the tart to the oven and bake for 20 mins until golden.
5. Leave to cool completely on a wire rack before filling.

Recommended fillings: lemon zest, mascarpone cream, maple pecan, any of the creamier fillings.

Walnut Shortcrust

65 MINS BAKED

INGREDIENTS

200G PLAIN FLOUR

100G UNSALTED BUTTER, CUBED

50G GROUND WALNUTS

1 TBSP CASTER SUGAR

1 EGG YOLK

METHOD

1. Rub the butter into the flour, sugar and ground walnuts until the mixture resembles fine breadcrumbs.
2. Add the egg yolk and a splash of cold water, bringing the dough together with a butter knife. Shape the dough into a disc before wrapping it in cling film and chilling for 30 mins.
3. Roll the dough out to approximately 5mm in thickness. Press it into the tart tin, leaving a little overhang at the edges. Poke the base several times with a fork and refrigerate for 15 mins.
4. Bake for 15–20 mins at 180°/160° (fan)/gas mark 4. Cool before filling.

Recommended fillings: pear and almond frangipane, spiced pumpkin custard, hazelnut praline, any of the cream cheese-based fillings.

Coconut Macaroon

40 MINS BAKED

Store-bought macaroons can be very sticky, but don't let them fool you into omitting the butter. It will all come together in the oven, trust me.

INGREDIENTS

380G STORE-BOUGHT COCONUT MACAROONS

50G UNSALTED BUTTER

METHOD

1. Preheat the oven to 180°/160° (fan)/gas mark 4.
2. Break down the macaroons to as fine a crumb as possible (this may be a little tricky as macaroons are notoriously moist).
3. Heat the butter in short bursts in the microwave and stir it into the macaroon mixture.
4. Press the macaroon butter mixture into the tart tin. Bake in the oven for 25 mins.
5. Leave the tart case to cool in its tin for at least 30 mins before removing. Store in an airtight container until you are ready to add the filling.

Maple Porridge Oat

45 MINS

BAKED

INGREDIENTS

200G ROLLED OATS

40G BUTTER, SOFTENED

3 TBSP MAPLE SYRUP

1 TSP GROUND CINNAMON

½ TSP GROUND GINGER

¼ TSP GROUND CLOVES

PINCH SALT

METHOD

1. Preheat the oven to 180°/160° (fan)/gas mark 4.
2. Combine all of the ingredients in a large bowl, stirring until well mixed.
3. Press the maple mixture into the tart tin, ensuring it is well compacted with no air pockets.
4. Bake for 20–25 mins. Leave to cool completely before removing from the tin.

Recommended fillings: maple pecan, coconut lime cream, chocolate ganache.

Chocolate Chip Cookie Dough

40 MINS BAKED OR CHILLED

INGREDIENTS

120G UNSALTED BUTTER, SOFTENED

120G SOFT LIGHT BROWN SUGAR

80G CASTER SUGAR

1 MEDIUM EGG (OR 2 TBSP MILK, IF KEEPING RAW)

1 TSP VANILLA EXTRACT

180G PLAIN FLOUR

½ TSP BICARBONATE OF SODA

½ TSP SALT

100G CHOCOLATE CHIPS

Tip: If the dough feels sticky while pressing it into the tin, pop it in the fridge for 15 mins first – it will firm up nicely and be easier to work with.

METHOD

1. Cream together the butter, brown sugar and caster sugar until pale, fluffy and well blended.
2. Beat in the egg and vanilla extract (or milk, if you'd rather keep the crust unbaked).
3. In a separate bowl, whisk together the flour, bicarbonate of soda and salt. Tip this into the butter mixture and stir until it just comes together as a dough.
4. Fold through the chocolate chips until evenly distributed.
5. Press the dough into the base and sides of your tart tin.
   - For a no-bake tart crust, chill for at least 1 hour before filling.
   - For a firmer baked case, chill the dough in the tin for 30 mins, then bake at 180°/160° (fan)/gas mark 4 for 10–12 mins, or until lightly golden. Allow to cool completely before filling.

Recommended fillings: cookie cheesecake, strawberry cream, marshmallow cream, or even a scoop of ice cream for a playful twist.

Basic Pastry

65 MINS BAKED

The key to good pastry is keeping it cool and handling it as little as possible. If you have particularly warm hands or are fortunate enough to live in warmer climes, try popping the bowl of flour and cubed butter in the freezer for 15 mins before you get down to business.

As always, I won't judge you if you opt for pre-packaged shortcrust pastry or even go as far as buying a pre-baked tart crust from a supermarket. Hell, I don't even care if you buy a frozen cheesecake and decorate that. If any part of the process stresses you out or fails to bring you joy, cheat. Buy the bits you don't like working on and enjoy the bits you do. I won't tell your mum, promise.

INGREDIENTS

200G PLAIN FLOUR

100G UNSALTED BUTTER, CHILLED AND CUBED

1–2 TBSP ICED WATER

FOR THE CHOCOLATE OPTION

15G COCOA

METHOD

1. In a large bowl, toss the cubed butter into the flour and salt. If it's chocolate pastry you're after, now is the time to add the cocoa.
2. Rub the flour into the butter with your fingertips until the mixture resembles fine breadcrumbs. Add a spoonful of iced water and give the mixture a good stir with a butter knife. If it seems a little dry, add another spoonful of water to ease it along.
3. Bring the pastry together with your hands, forming it into a chunky disc. Wrap in clingfilm and refrigerate for 30 mins.
4. Preheat the oven to 180°/160° (fan)/gas mark 4. Take the pastry out of the fridge and roll it out to a thickness of approximately 5mm. You may need a little flour to prevent the pastry sticking to the worktop, but do try to keep it to a minimum.
5. Transfer the pastry to the tart tin, carefully pressing it into the ridges. If it tears a little along the way, don't worry, just use a piece of offcut to patch it up.
6. Trim the excess pastry so it sits no higher than 5mm over the edges of the tin. Prick the base of the pastry case with a fork and refrigerate for a further 15 mins.
7. Place a sheet of baking paper in the base of the tart tin and fill with baking beans or dry, uncooked rice. Bake for 10 mins before removing the beans/rice and paper. Return to the oven and bake for a further 5 mins.
8. Transfer the tin to a wire rack and quickly trim any excess pastry from the edges. Leave to cool fully before removing from the tin.

Popcorn and Toffee Nut

2 HOURS CHILLED

INGREDIENTS

100G POPCORN

50G TOFFEE PIECES OR 50G TOFFEES, SMASHED INTO SHARDS

50G HAZELNUTS, CHOPPED

60G BUTTER, MELTED

METHOD

1. Lightly crush the popcorn (don't completely obliterate it, think chocolate-chip sized pieces).
2. Toss the toffee pieces and hazelnuts into the popcorn mixture and give it a good stir.
3. Add the melted butter, making sure everything is well covered.
4. Transfer the mixture to the tart tin, compacting it into the base and sides as much as possible. Refrigerate for 1.5 hours, or until set.

Recommended fillings: mascarpone cream, chocolate caramel ganache, anything sweet.

Matcha and Almond

75 MINS BAKED

INGREDIENTS

150G PLAIN FLOUR

50G GROUND ALMONDS

2 TSP MATCHA POWDER

100G UNSALTED BUTTER, CUBED

50G SUGAR

1 EGG YOLK

METHOD

1. Combine the flour, ground almonds and matcha in a large bowl. Rub in the butter with your fingertips until the mixture resembles coarse breadcrumbs.
2. Add the sugar and the egg yolk, stirring to form a soft dough.
3. Wrap the dough in cling film and press it into a large disc. Chill for 30 mins.
4. Roll the pastry out on a lightly floured worktop and carefully transfer it to the tin. Prick the base several times with a fork before returning the tin to the fridge for a further 15 mins.
5. Preheat the oven to 180°/160° (fan)/ gas mark 4 while the pastry is chilling.
6. Bake in the oven for 20–25 mins, or until crisp. Leave to cool completely before removing from the tin.

Recommended fillings: honey lavender cream, coconut lime cream, dark chocolate ganache.

Pine Nut Shortcrust

65 MINS BAKED

INGREDIENTS

200G FLOUR

60G PINE NUTS, FINELY CHOPPED

100G BUTTER, CUBED AND CHILLED

1 EGG YOLK

METHOD

1. Preheat the oven to 180°/160° (fan)/gas mark 4.
2. Combine the flour and butter, rubbing them together with your fingertips. Stir in the chopped pine nuts.
3. Add the yolk, stirring to form a soft dough. Wrap it in cling film and refrigerate for 30 mins.
4. Roll the pastry out onto a lightly floured worktop before transferring it to the tart tin. Bake for 18–20 mins, or until golden and crisp.

Recommended fillings: honey lavender cream, apricot almond cream, salted caramel, thyme custard.

Choc-cherry Granola

15 MINS CHILLED

INGREDIENTS

150g chocolate granola

50g glacé cherries

40g butter, melted

METHOD

1. Chop the glacé cherries into quarters (you can do this with clean kitchen scissors if you prefer).
2. Give the granola a light bash if it's a little chunky. Stir in the cherries.
3. Melt the butter over a medium heat and stir it into the granola mix. Spoon it into the tart tin and compress using the back of a spoon.
4. Refrigerate for 1 hour, or until fully set.

Recommended fillings: chocolate ganache, mascarpone cream.

Hazelnut Shortcrust

60 MINS BAKED

INGREDIENTS

200G PLAIN FLOUR

100G BUTTER, CHILLED AND CUBED

50G GROUND HAZELNUTS

50G SUGAR

METHOD

1. Preheat the oven to 180°/160° (fan)/gas mark 4.
2. Sift together the flour and ground hazelnuts. Stir in the sugar.
3. Rub in the butter, being careful not to overwork the mixture.
4. Roll the pastry out and use it to line your tart tin. Prick the base several times with a fork and refrigerate for 15 mins.
5. Fill the tart case with a sheet of baking paper topped with baking beans or uncooked rice. Bake for 10 mins.
6. Remove the paper and baking beans and return the tart to the oven for a further 10 mins. Leave to cool completely before filling.

Recommended fillings: chocolate ganache, thyme custard, hazelnut praline cream.

Gingerbread

60 MINS BAKED

INGREDIENTS

200G PLAIN FLOUR

83G UNSALTED BUTTER

66G SOFT DARK BROWN SUGAR

1 TBSP GOLDEN SYRUP

¼ TSP BICARBONATE OF SODA

2 TSP GROUND GINGER

METHOD

1. Preheat the oven to 200°/180° (fan)/gas mark 6.
2. Stir together the flour, ground ginger and bicarbonate of soda. Set the bowl aside.
3. In a small pan over a medium heat, gently melt the sugar, golden syrup and butter. Keep stirring until you have a dark, glossy syrup.
4. Remove the pan from the heat and pour the syrup mixture into the flour. Give it a good stir until you have a soft, squidgy dough.
5. Turn the dough out onto a sheet of baking/greaseproof paper (try not to miss this step, it will be a rascal to manage otherwise). Roll the dough out to approximately 5mm in thickness. In one quick motion, take the two edges of the dough-covered paper and flip it over into the tart tin. Gingerbread is fabulously pliable, so you can patch and add as you go if your flip fails.
6. Remove the paper and press the dough into the tin. Prick the base with a fork and refrigerate for 15 mins.
7. Bake the gingerbread case in the oven for 15–20 mins, or until both the edges and base are crisp and golden. Transfer to a wire rack and swiftly trim off any excess gingerbread. Gobble up any offcuts while warm, leaving the tart to cool completely before filling.

Pistachio

70 MINS BAKED

INGREDIENTS

340G PISTACHIOS (SHELLED WEIGHT)

50G CASTER SUGAR

30G UNSALTED BUTTER

¼ TSP SALT

1 EGG

Tip: Try switching out the pistachios for hazelnuts or cashews.

METHOD

1. Blitz the pistachios in a food processor until smooth. Alternatively, place them in a sandwich bag, cover with a tea towel, and channel all your rage into bashing them into bits with a rolling pin. Whatever floats your boat.
2. Rub the butter into the ground pistachios. Stir in the salt, caster sugar and egg to form a sticky dough. Wrap the dough in cling film and refrigerate for 30 mins.
3. Preheat the oven to 180°/160° (fan)/gas mark 4.
4. Roll the dough out onto a lightly floured worktop. Transfer to the tart tin and prick the base several times with a fork. Refrigerate for a further 15 mins.
5. Bake the tart case in the preheated oven for 20–25 mins, or until the edges begin to crisp. Leave to cook completely on a wire rack.

Puffed Quinoa Chocolate

70 MINS CHILLED

INGREDIENTS

100G PUFFED QUINOA

50G COCOA POWDER

70G CASTER SUGAR

60G UNSALTED BUTTER, MELTED

METHOD

1. In a large bowl, mix together the puffed quinoa, cocoa powder and caster sugar.
2. Melt the butter over a medium heat. Add it to the dry ingredients, stirring until well covered.
3. Spoon the mixture into the tart tin, pressing it down using the back of a spoon. Refrigerate for at least an hour, or until fully set.

Recommended fillings: chocolate caramel ganache, espresso chocolate mousse.

Tip: This is a crust that carries additions well: chocolate chips, crushed nuts, chopped honeycomb, just stir them in before pressing the mixture into the tin.

Churro Doughnut

45 MINS BAKED

INGREDIENTS

150G PLAIN FLOUR

50G CASTER SUGAR

50G UNSALTED BUTTER

1 TSP CINNAMON

1 EGG YOLK

PINCH SALT

FOR THE TIN

20G UNSALTED BUTTER

50G SUGAR

METHOD

1. Preheat the oven to 180°/160° (fan)/ gas mark 4.
2. Rub the butter into the flour, sugar, cinnamon and salt.
3. Add the egg yolk, using a butter knife to bring the dough together. Wrap it in cling film and chill for 30 mins.
4. Melt the extra butter over a low heat.
5. Cover the inside of the tin in melted butter. Add the sugar and give it a good shake, ensuring it is well covered. Tip out any excess and pop the tin in the fridge for 15 mins.
6. Roll the dough out onto a lightly floured worktop. Transfer to the sugared tart tin and prick the base several times with a fork. Chill for a further 15 mins.
7. Bake for 20–25 mins, or until golden. Leave to cool completely before removing from the tin.

Recommended fillings: spiced pumpkin custard, maple pecan.

INGREDIENTS

120G CORNFLAKES, SLIGHTLY CRUSHED

160G MARS BARS, CHOPPED

2 TBSP MILK

2.5 HOURS

CHILLED

Chocolate Caramel Cornflake

METHOD

1. Heat a little water in a pan on the hob. Place the chopped Mars bars and milk in a heatproof bowl and place it on top of the pan, making sure the base of the bowl doesn't touch the water. Stir the mixture until it has loosened into a smooth, chocolatey caramel goo.
2. Remove the bowl from the simmering pan and stir in the crushed cornflakes. Spoon the mixture into the tart tin, using the back of a spoon to ease it into the ridges and base. Leave to set in the fridge for at least 2 hours before using.

Rye and Cocoa

65 MINS BAKED

INGREDIENTS

150G PLAIN FLOUR

50G RYE FLOUR

25G COCOA POWDER

100G UNSALTED BUTTER, CUBED AND CHILLED

50G CASTER SUGAR

1 EGG YOLK

METHOD

1. Combine the plain and rye flours in a large bowl. Add the chilled butter and rub it in using the tips of your fingers.
2. Add the egg yolk and bring the dough together using a butter knife. Wrap the dough in cling film and chill for 30 mins.
3. Roll the pastry out to a thickness of 5mm. Carefully transfer it to the tin, pressing it into the sides.
4. Preheat the oven to180°/160° (fan)/gas mark 4.
5. Place a sheet of baking paper inside the pastry case and fill with baking beans or uncooked rice. Chill for a further 15 mins.
6. Bake for 15 mins. Remove the paper and baking beans/rice from the tart and bake for a further 10 mins.
7. Leave to cool completely before removing from the tin.

Recommended fillings: dark chocolate and raspberry swirl, spiced blackberry custard.

Peanut Butter Cookie

40 MINS   BAKED

INGREDIENTS

150G PLAIN FLOUR

100G PEANUT BUTTER

50G CASTER SUGAR

50G UNSALTED BUTTER, MELTED

1 EGG

METHOD

1. Preheat the oven to 180°/160° (fan)/ gas mark 4.
2. Mix all the ingredients until a soft dough forms.
3. As the dough is very soft, it is easier to spoon it into the tart tin and press it into place with your fingers. Poke some holes in the base with a fork and refrigerate for 30 mins.
4. Bake for 18–22 mins, or until the pastry is crisp and golden.
5. Leave to cool completely before filling.

Recommended fillings: banana cream, mascarpone cream, caramelised pineapple cream.

Lemon and Lime

75 MINS

BAKED

INGREDIENTS

66G CASTER SUGAR

2 TSP LEMON ZEST

1 TSP LIME ZEST

190G PLAIN FLOUR

¼ TSP SALT

112G UNSALTED BUTTER, CHILLED AND CUBED

1 EGG

1–2 TBSP CHILLED WATER

METHOD

1. Toss the cubed butter into the flour, salt and zest, giving the bowl a good shake.
2. Using the tips of your fingers, rub the butter into the dry ingredients. Stir in the egg to form a soft pastry. If the mixture seems a little dry, add a spoonful or two of water to bring it together.
3. Wrap the dough in cling film and refrigerate for 30 mins. Meanwhile, preheat the oven to 190°/170° (fan)/gas mark 5.
4. Turn the dough out onto a worktop and roll it out to approximately 5mm in thickness. Carefully transfer the pastry to the tart tin. Prick the base with a fork and refrigerate for 15 mins.
5. Cover the base of the tart with a sheet of baking paper and fill with baking beans/uncooked rice. Bake for 14 mins before removing the paper and beans/rice, and baking for a further 7 mins. Leave the pastry to cool completely before removing it from the tin.

Chocolate Digestive

1 HOUR CHILLED

INGREDIENTS

200G CHOCOLATE DIGESTIVES

50G COCOA POWDER

75G UNSALTED BUTTER, MELTED

Tip: There's a multitude of flavoured chocolate digestives on the market now: white chocolate, golden chocolate, even gingerbread with dark chocolate. Feel free to try a something different for a fun twist.

METHOD

1. Blitz the digestives into crumbs in a food processor or pop them in a bag and give them a good going over with a rolling pin.
2. Stir in cocoa powder and melted butter, ensuring the crumbs are evenly coated.
3. Tip the biscuit mix directly into the tart tin and press it firmly into the base and sides. For a super-smooth finish, running the base of a shot glass over the crust will help even out the edges.
4. Refrigerate for at least 20 mins.

Recommended fillings: chocolate caramel ganache, mocha cheesecake.

Polenta and Honey

50 MINS BAKED

INGREDIENTS

150G PLAIN FLOUR

50G POLENTA

70G UNSALTED BUTTER, MELTED

3 TBSP CLEAR HONEY

1 TBSP CASTER SUGAR

METHOD

1. Preheat the oven to 180°/160° (fan)/gas mark 4.
2. In a large bowl, combine the flour, polenta and sugar. Stir in the butter and honey to create a soft, pliable dough.
3. Wrap the dough in cling film and roll into a cylinder. Refrigerate for 20 mins.
4. Remove the dough from the fridge and slice it into discs approximately 5mm thick. Press the discs into the tin, making sure to cover all gaps. Bake for 20–25 mins until golden brown.
5. Leave to cool completely on a wire rack before filling.

Recommended fillings: lemon and lime, mascarpone cream, caramelised pineapple cream.

Sesame Sugar Snap

30 MINS BAKED

INGREDIENTS

200G SESAME SEEDS

120G CASTER SUGAR

80G UNSALTED BUTTER

Tip: This is a delicate crust, so be super careful when removing it from the tin.

METHOD

1. Preheat the oven to 180°/160° (fan)/gas mark 4.
2. Melt the butter and sugar together over a low heat. We want it to be pale and golden rather than caramelised.
3. Remove the pan from the heat and stir in the sesame seeds.
4. Pour the mixture into the tart tin and press down evenly using the back of a spoon. Bake for 12–16 mins, or until crisp.
5. Cool on a wire rack.

Recommended fillings: honey lavender cream, coconut lime cream, anything soft and silky.

Salted Pretzel

30 MINS

BAKED

INGREDIENTS

125G SALTED PRETZELS

25G ICING SUGAR

30G PLAIN FLOUR

85G UNSALTED BUTTER, SOFTENED

1 EGG YOLK

METHOD

1. Preheat the oven to 180°/160° (fan)/gas mark 4.
2. Using a food processor or a heavy serving of elbow grease, blitz the pretzels to crumbs.
3. Stir in the icing sugar, flour, softened butter and egg yolk, mixing until well combined.
4. Spoon the pretzel mixture into the tart tin, pressing it into the sides and base with the back of a spoon.
5. Bake the case in the oven for 25 mins before leaving to cool completely on a wire rack.

Tip: If the case slumps a little during the bake, just press it back up the sides of the tin with a spoon before cooling. It will remain fairly pliable until it is fully cool.

Golden Syrup Flapjack

35 MINS BAKED

INGREDIENTS

150G ROLLED OATS

50G PLAIN FLOUR

60G GOLDEN SYRUP

40G BUTTER

40G BROWN SUGAR

METHOD

1. Preheat the oven to 180°/160° (fan)/ gas mark 4.
2. In a medium-sized pan, melt the golden syrup, butter and sugar over a low heat.
3. Remove the pan from the hob and place on a heat-safe surface. Stir in the oats and the flour.
4. Tip this gloriously scented mixture into the tart tin and press it into the sides. Bake for 20 mins until golden.

Recommended fillings: lemon zest, mascarpone cream, banana cream, pretty much any cold (no-bake) filling would be delicious.

Caramel Chocolate Case

15 mins   Chilled

INGREDIENTS

250G CARAMEL FLAVOURED CHOCOLATE

METHOD

1. Line the base of your tart tin with a circle of greaseproof paper.
2. Chop the chocolate into small pieces. Place it in a heatproof bowl on top of a pan of barely simmering water.
3. Gently stir the chocolate to speed up the melting time. Ideally, you want the chocolate to melt into itself without getting too hot. Once there are only a few lumps left, remove the bowl and continue to mix off the heat until the chocolate has fully melted. Leave to stand for 3 mins.
4. Pour half of the chocolate into the tart tin. Using a pastry brush, work it up the sides until fully coated. Repeat with the remaining chocolate.
5. Refrigerate until fully set. If you struggle to get the case out of the tin, dip the base in a shallow tray of warm water (making sure not to get the chocolate wet) and try again.

Recommended fillings: white chocolate and pistachio ganache, apricot almond cream; nothing from the baked section, for obvious reasons.

Speculoos Biscuit and White Chocolate Chip

30 MINS CHILLED

INGREDIENTS

250G SPECULOOS BISCUITS, CRUSHED

50G WHITE CHOCOLATE CHIPS

60G BUTTER, MELTED

METHOD

1. Smash the biscuits to smithereens. Stir in the white chocolate chips.
2. Melt the butter over a low heat before adding it to the biscuit mixture.
3. Press the mixture into the tart tin as evenly as possible. Refrigerate for at least an hour before filling.

Recommended fillings: mascarpone cream, banana cream, anything sweet and cold.

Oreo Cookie

OVERNIGHT CHILLED

INGREDIENTS

250G OREO COOKIES

40G MELTED BUTTER

METHOD

1. Place the Oreo cookies in a sandwich bag and cover with a tea towel. Go over the towel several times with a rolling pin until the biscuits are well crushed. You can also use a food processor for this step but be mindful that this mixture gets claggy pretty quickly.
2. Toss the crushed biscuits into a bowl and stir in the melted butter. Transfer the mixture to the tart tin and press firmly with the back of a spoon. Refrigerate overnight before filling.

TIp: You can use pretty much any variety of filled biscuit for this recipe: custard creams and bourbons work particularly well. Jammy Dodgers can get a bit sticky but are well worth the extra cleaning time.

Basic Biscuit

2.5 HOURS

CHILLED

INGREDIENTS

250G DIGESTIVE/ GINGER/SHORTBREAD BISCUITS

50G GOLDEN CASTER SUGAR

60G UNSALTED BUTTER, MELTED

METHOD

1. Bash the biscuits into crumbs. Add the golden caster sugar and melted butter, stirring until soft and sticky.
2. Spoon the biscuit mixture into the tart tin and press firmly into the edges and base. Refrigerate until set, preferably overnight.
3. Carefully remove the base from the tin and fill 'er up.

The Fillings

Fill 'Em Up

Now it's time to get cracking on the gooey, silky, creamy loveliness that is the filling. Some are refrigerated, some are baked, all are delicious. Feel free to mix and match as you please.

If this is your first foray into desserts, then I'd recommend you start with the mascarpone cream filling (p. 71): it is so thick that you could technically decorate over it right away (although I would certainly advise you give it at least a couple of hours in the fridge beforehand). The marshmallow cream filling (p. 68) is another great confidence builder, as the gelatine in the marshmallows acts as a built-in setting agent and does all the heavy lifting for you. Both are excellent starting points for the nervous cook.

On first appearances, the baked fillings may seem like a bit of a faff compared to the chilled options, but the beauty of the baked is that you can decorate (and more importantly, eat) them far sooner. If you are a first timer, try the thyme baked custard. It is straightforward and, if you're careful with the heat, never fails.

Finally, OK, I get it, sometimes you're short on time and patience. Hey, that's fine by me, feel free to buy a cheesecake from the supermarket and skip to next chapter. Go with whatever makes your soul happy.

Thyme Custard

65 MINS   BAKED

INGREDIENTS

200ML DOUBLE CREAM

200ML MILK

1 VANILLA POD

3 STEMS OF FRESH THYME

6 EGG YOLKS

80G CASTER SUGAR

¼ TSP GRATED NUTMEG

Tip: If your custard splits, place the pan in a shallow basin of cold water and whisk vigorously until it comes back together.

METHOD

1. Preheat the oven to 140°/120° (fan)/ gas mark 1.
2. Whisk together the egg yolks and caster sugar until pale and fluffy. Set aside.
3. Combine the cream and milk in a saucepan. Scrape out the vanilla pod and toss the seeds, empty pod, thyme and nutmeg into the milk. Gently heat for 3–5 mins, or until the liquid has reduced by a third.
4. Carefully remove the thyme stems and vanilla pod. Pour the liquid over the egg and sugar mixture, whisking until smooth and glossy.
5. Pour the custard into your prepared tart tin and bake in the oven for 55 mins. Any hint of wobble should set as the filling cools.

Recommended crusts: chocolate pastry, gingerbread, pistachio.

Marshmallow Cream

2 HOURS   CHILLED

INGREDIENTS

100G WHITE MARSHMALLOWS

15ML MILK

260ML DOUBLE CREAM

1 TSP VANILLA EXTRACT

METHOD

1. Pop the marshmallows and milk in a pan. Heat, stirring continuously, until fully melted. Remove the pan from the stove and leave to cool for a few minutes while you prepare the cream.
2. Whip the cream and vanilla extracts until soft peaks form. Fold half of the marshmallow mixture into the whipped cream until well combined. Repeat with the second half, being careful not to beat too much air out of the marshmallow cream.
3. Spoon the filling into your prepared tart case and refrigerate until set (this should take approximately 2 hours).

Recommended crusts: any at all – this classic filling is a beautiful all-rounder, perfect for both sweet and salty crusts.

Maple Pecan

2 HOURS CHILLED

INGREDIENTS

200ML DOUBLE CREAM

150G CREAM CHEESE

50G MAPLE SYRUP

50G CHOPPED PECANS

METHOD

1. Whip the cream until soft peaks form.
2. Beat the cream cheese and maple syrup until silky smooth.
3. Fold the cream into the maple cream cheese mixture.
4. Stir in chopped pecans. Spoon into tart case and chill for 2 hours.

Recommended crusts: almond, basic biscuit, walnut shortcrust, candied pecan.

Raspberry Ripple Cream

2 HOURS CHILLED

INGREDIENTS

200ML DOUBLE CREAM

200G MASCARPONE

100G RASPBERRIES

50G ICING SUGAR

Tip: It would be a terrible shame to cover the marbling effect. Rather than spending your time decorating, just top with a stack of fresh raspberries and a dusting of icing sugar.

METHOD

1. Whip the cream and icing sugar to soft peaks. Gently fold in the mascarpone.
2. Swirl in mashed raspberries without fully mixing for a ripple effect.
3. Spoon into tart case, running a toothpick or skewer over the top to enhance the marble effect.
4. Chill for 2–3 hours.

Recommended crusts: Oreo cookie, basic biscuit, chocolate digestives.

Espresso Chocolate Mousse

3 HOURS CHILLED

INGREDIENTS

200G DARK CHOCOLATE, CHOPPED

250ML DOUBLE CREAM

2 TBSP ESPRESSO

3 EGG YOLKS

25G CASTER SUGAR

METHOD

1. Melt chocolate in a heatproof bowl suspended over a pan of simmering water.
2. Stir in the espresso.
3. In a separate bowl, whisk the yolks and caster sugar until fluffy.
4. Slowly pour the chocolate into the yolk and sugar mixture, being sure to fold it in gently.
5. Whip the cream to soft peaks and fold in chocolate mixture a little at a time. Try not to knock too much air out of the mousse as you go.
6. Spoon into tart case and chill at least 3 hours.

Recommended crusts: chocolate digestives, churro doughnut, basic biscuit.

Tip: This filling acts as a beautiful standalone recipe, sans tart. Leave to set in coupe glasses (those with a shallow, saucer-like bowl and a short stem) and serve with a dusting of cocoa powder.

Mascarpone Cream

2 HOURS CHILLED

INGREDIENTS

115G MASCARPONE CHEESE

40G CASTER SUGAR

285ML DOUBLE CREAM

1 TSP VANILLA EXTRACT

METHOD

1. Whisk together the mascarpone cheese, caster sugar and vanilla extract.
2. In a separate bowl, whip the double cream until soft peaks have formed.
3. Gently fold the mascarpone cheese mixture into the whipped cream, being careful not to knock out too much of the air.
4. Transfer the mixture to the tart tin and refrigerate for 2-6 hours before decorating.

Recommended crusts: pretzel, basic biscuit, lemon and lime, coconut macaroon, pistachio, chocolate, plain pastry.

Chocolate Caramel Ganache

4.5 HOURS CHILLED

INGREDIENTS

340G DARK CHOCOLATE, CHOPPED

200ML DOUBLE CREAM

60G UNSALTED BUTTER

200G TINNED CARAMEL

METHOD

1. Spoon the caramel into your prepared tart case. Refrigerate for 30 mins.
2. Place the chopped chocolate in a large bowl and set aside. Heat the cream until it is close to boiling point (the edges will start to bubble a little).
3. Pour the hot cream over the chocolate and leave to work its magic for 2 mins.
4. Add the butter to the chocolate and cream mixture and whisk until smooth. If the chocolate hasn't melted completely, pop the bowl over a pan of barely simmering water and stir continuously until the mixture is free of any pesky lumps and bumps.
5. Pour the ganache into the caramel filled tart. Leave to cool for 4–6 hours before decorating.

Recommended crusts: chocolate caramel, cornflake chocolate pastry, Oreo cookie, pretzel.

Banoffee Cream

2.5 HOURS CHILLED

INGREDIENTS

2 RIPE BANANAS, SLICED

200ML DOUBLE CREAM

150G MASCARPONE

2 TBSP GOLDEN SYRUP

METHOD

1. Whip the cream to soft peaks.
2. Fold in the mascarpone and golden syrup, being careful not to over-soften the whipped cream.
3. Layer the banana slices in the tart case. Slowly pour the cream mixture over the top.
4. Chill for 2 hours

Recommended crusts: basic biscuit, salted pretzel, almond, churro doughnut.

Pear and Almond Frangipane

1.5 HOURS BAKED

INGREDIENTS

100G UNSALTED BUTTER, SOFTENED

100G SUGAR

2 EGGS

100G GROUND ALMONDS

50G PLAIN FLOUR

1-2 PEARS, SLICED THINLY

METHOD

1. Beat the butter and sugar until pale and fluffy.
2. Add eggs, one at a time, mixing well between additions. If the mixture looks like it's splitting, add a spoonful of the allocated flour before adding the next egg.
3. Fold in the ground almonds and plain flour.
4. Arrange pears in tart case before pouring the frangipane over the top.
5. Bake for 35-40 mins at 180°/160° (fan)/ gas mark 4.
6. Leave to cool completely.

Recommended crusts: almond, walnut shortcrust, gingerbread.

Tip: Another tart that sings on its own, no decoration required. Slice it up warm, topping each segment with a scoop of rich vanilla ice cream.

Honey Lavender Cream

2 HOURS   CHILLED

INGREDIENTS

250ML DOUBLE CREAM

150G CREAM CHEESE

2 TBSP HONEY

1 TSP DRIED LAVENDER

METHOD

1. Whip the cream to soft peaks.
2. Beat together the cream cheese with honey and lavender.
3. Fold the decadently fragrant cream cheese mixture into the whipped cream a third at a time.
4. Spoon the filling into the tart case and chill for 2 hours before serving.

Recommended crusts: gingerbread, coconut macaroon, pistachio.

Tip: A few sprigs of fresh lavender are all you need to decorate this delicious tart. Pair with the gingerbread crust for a stunning dessert.

Amaretto and White Chocolate

4 HOURS CHILLED

INGREDIENTS

120G WHITE CHOCOLATE, CHOPPED

1 TBSP AMARETTO OR ALMOND EXTRACT

2 MEDIUM EGGS, SEPARATED

200ML DOUBLE CREAM

45G CASTER SUGAR

METHOD

1. Melt the white chocolate, either in short bursts in the microwave or in a heatproof dish over a pan of barely simmering water.
2. Stir in the amaretto/almond extract and egg yolks.
3. Beat the egg whites until white, fluffy and almost double in volume. Add the sugar a spoonful at a time, beating between additions.
4. Fold half of the egg mixture into the melted chocolate before repeating with the other half. Gently transfer the mousse mixture into the tart case and refrigerate for 4–6 hours.

Recommended crusts: basic biscuit, almond, chocolate pastry, pretzel, plain pastry.

Lemon Zest

70 mins   Baked

INGREDIENTS

4 MEDIUM EGGS PLUS 2 EXTRA YOLKS

150G CASTER SUGAR

JUICE OF 2 LEMONS

ZEST OF 4 LEMONS

200ML DOUBLE CREAM

METHOD

1. Preheat the oven to 140°/120° (fan)/gas mark 2.
2. Whisk all of the ingredients together in a large bowl. A hand whisk is fine for this filling, it doesn't require as much gusto as the chilled ones.
3. Carefully pour the mixture into the tart case. Bake in the oven for 45–55 mins, or until the filling is firm on top with the slightest hint of wobble in the centre.
4. Place the tart on a wire rack and leave to cool completely before removing the tin.

Recommended crusts: lemon and lime, basic pastry and (slightly controversially) any of the chocolate-based tart cases.

Mango and Passionfruit Curd

45 MINS   CHILLED

INGREDIENTS

200G MANGO PURÉE

100ML PASSIONFRUIT PULP

3 EGGS

80G CASTER SUGAR

50G BUTTER

METHOD

1. In a medium-sized pan, gently heat the mango purée, passionfruit pulp and caster sugar. Remove the pan from the heat once the sugar has dissolved, leaving to cool ever so slightly.
2. Beat the eggs in a jug. Slowly pour them into the fruit mixture, whisking continuously.
3. Cook until the mixture has thickened and reduced by just over a third. Remove the pan from the heat and stir in the butter until glossy.
4. Pour the mixture into tart case. Chill for 2 hours, or preferably overnight.

Recommended crusts: almond, basic biscuit, coconut macaroon.

Hazelnut Praline Cream

2 HOURS CHILLED

INGREDIENTS

200ML DOUBLE CREAM

100G MASCARPONE

50G HAZELNUT PRALINE PASTE

METHOD

1. Whip the cream until soft peaks form.
2. In a separate bowl, fold the mascarpone and praline paste together.
3. Add one third of the praline mixture to the whipped cream, folding until fully incorporated. Repeat with the remaining two thirds.
4. Spoon the filling into tart case and chill for 2 hours.

Recommended crusts: pistachio, chocolate digestives, walnut shortcrust, churro doughnut.

Spiced Pumpkin Custard

60 MINS BAKED

INGREDIENTS

200G PUMPKIN PURÉE

200ML MILK

100ML DOUBLE CREAM

3 EGGS

50G CASTER SUGAR

1 TSP CINNAMON

½ TSP NUTMEG

METHOD

1. Preheat the oven to 160°/140° (fan)/gas mark 3.
2. Whisk together the eggs and sugar until pale and fluffy.
3. Heat the milk, cream and spices in a medium saucepan until the edges start to bubble ever so slightly. Remove the pan from the hob and leave to cool for 3 mins.
4. In a separate bowl, whisk the eggs until golden amber. Pour a small amount of the spice mixture into the eggs, whisking continuously. Add the rest, making sure to whisk while pouring.
5. Stir in the pumpkin purée. Carefully pour the filling into the tart case.
6. Bake for 40–45 mins, or until there's only the slightest hint of wobble in the centre of the tart. Leave to cool completely before decorating/serving.

Recommended crusts: gingerbread, almond, basic pastry, bran flake.

Cherry Clafoutis

50 MINS BAKED

INGREDIENTS

150G PITTED CHERRIES

3 EGGS

100ML MILK

100ML CREAM

50G CASTER SUGAR

25G PLAIN FLOUR

METHOD

1. Preheat the oven 180°/160° (fan)/gas mark 4.
2. Whisk together the eggs, sugar, flour, milk and cream until smooth.
3. Scatter the cherries in the tart case. Pour the custard mixture over the top.
4. Bake for 30–35 mins until set. Leave to cool completely before decorating.

Recommended crusts: almond, basic pastry, chocolate.

Tip: To save transporting a custard-laden tart from worktop to oven, have your cherry-filled tart case ready on the oven shelf before pouring the custard mixture over the top. Less stress, less spillage.

Spiced Blackberry Custard

60 MINS BAKED

INGREDIENTS

200ML DOUBLE CREAM

200ML WHOLE MILK

6 EGG YOLKS

80G SOFT DARK BROWN SUGAR

1 TSP GROUND CINNAMON

½ TSP GROUND GINGER

¼ TSP NUTMEG

100G BLACKBERRIES

METHOD

1. Preheat the oven to 140°/120° (fan)/ gas mark 1.
2. Combine the double cream, whole milk and spices in a medium-sized pan. Bring to a boil before setting the pan aside to cool for 2 mins.
3. Beat together the egg yolks and sugar. Carefully pour the hot liquid into the egg mixture, whisking until smooth.
4. Scatter the blackberries in the base of you chosen pastry case. Top with the custard and bake in the oven for 40 mins. Leave to cool completely before decorating.

Recommended crusts: basic pastry, almond, or pistachio; maybe pretzel, if you are feeling a little adventurous.

Cookie Cheesecake

2.5 HOURS CHILLED

INGREDIENTS

180G CREAM CHEESE

50G ICING SUGAR

1 TSP VANILLA EXTRACT

190ML DOUBLE CREAM

12 CHOCOLATE CHIP COOKIES/OREOS, CHOPPED

METHOD

1. Whisk the cream cheese and vanilla extract until smooth and glossy.
2. In a separate bowl, whisk the double cream and icing sugar until thick and softly peaked.
3. Gently fold a third of the cream cheese mixture into the cream until fully incorporated. Repeat a further two times.
4. Stir the chopped cookies into the cheesecake mixture. Scoop the filling into the tart case, smoothing it in with the back of a spoon.
5. Refrigerate for at least 2 hours before decorating.

Recommended crusts: Oreo cookie, marshmallow cereal, basic biscuit, pretzel, either of the plain pastry cases.

Tip: You can use the same beaters for both the whipped cream and the cream cheese. You don't want to ruin your fun baking session with an unwanted mid-mix wash-up, just switch bowls and crack on.

Mocha Cheesecake

3 HOURS CHILLED

INGREDIENTS

200G CREAM CHEESE

100G CASTER SUGAR

150ML DOUBLE CREAM

2 TBSP COFFEE (POWDERED)

METHOD

1. Whisk together the cream cheese and caster sugar until smooth.
2. In a separate bowl, whip the cream and coffee until soft peaks form.
3. Fold the whipped coffee cream into the cream cheese mixture.
4. Spoon the mocha cheesecake mousse into the tart case, Smooth with a palette knife. Leave to chill for 2 hours.

Recommended crusts: Oreo cookie, chocolate digestives, churro doughnut, hazelnut pastry.

Apple Crumble Custard

1 HOUR BAKED

INGREDIENTS

2 APPLES, PEELED AND CHOPPED

100G SUGAR

1 TSP CINNAMON

200ML MILK

100ML DOUBLE CREAM

2 EGGS

20G FLOUR

METHOD

1. Preheat the oven to 180°/160° (fan)/gas mark 4.
2. Toss the apples in a bowl along with the sugar and cinnamon. Scatter across the tart case.
3. Whisk the eggs, milk, cream and flour. Pour the custard over the apples.
4. Bake in the oven for 35–40 mins, or until the custard seems relatively set. Leave to cool completely before decorating.

Recommended crusts: basic pastry, gingerbread, almond.

Pistachio Cream and Rose

2 HOURS CHILLED

INGREDIENTS

200ML DOUBLE CREAM

150G MASCARPONE

50G PISTACHIO PASTE

½ TSP ROSE WATER

METHOD

1. Whip the cream to soft peaks.
2. Gently fold in the mascarpone, pistachio paste and rose water.
3. Spoon the filling into the tart case. Refrigerate for 2 hours.

Recommended crusts: pistachio, almond, chocolate digestive, basic pastry, chocolate.

Caramelised Pineapple Cream

2 HOURS CHILLED

INGREDIENTS

150G PINEAPPLE, CHOPPED

30G BUTTER

3 TBSP SOFT BROWN SUGAR

200ML DOUBLE CREAM

150G MASCARPONE

METHOD

1. Heat the butter in a deep frying pan. Add the brown sugar, stirring until dissolved.
2. Place the pineapple slices in the pan. Add a splash of rum, if you're so inclined. Cook for 3 mins on each side before leaving to cool.
3. Whip the cream to soft peaks.
4. Fold in the mascarpone and pineapple chunks.
5. Spoon the filling into the tart case. Refrigerate for 2 hours before decorating/serving.

Recommended crusts: basic biscuit, almond, coconut macaroon.

Strawberry Cream

Tip: This recipe is compatible with plenty of other fruits: raspberries, blackberries and cherries are all excellent alternatives for strawberries, if they're not your jam (I couldn't resist, sorry).

2 HOURS

CHILLED

INGREDIENTS

150G STRAWBERRIES, HULLED

105G ICING SUGAR

360ML DOUBLE CREAM

METHOD

1. Purée the strawberries by blitzing them in a food processor or giving them a bloody good mash with a fork.
2. Whip the cream and icing sugar until smooth, glossy and thick.
3. Fold in the strawberry purée to create a blushing-pink cream filling.
4. Dollop the mixture into the tart case and smooth with a palette knife or the back or a spoon. Refrigerate for 2 hours before decorating.

Recommended crusts: basic biscuit, marshmallow cereal, pretzel, either of the plain pastry cases.

Peachberry Custard

45 MINS

BAKED

INGREDIENTS

200G CASTER SUGAR

120ML DOUBLE CREAM

30G PLAIN FLOUR

2 MEDIUM EGGS

1 SMALL TIN OF PEACH SLICES

60G RASPBERRIES

METHOD

1. Preheat the oven to 180°/160° (fan)/gas mark 4.
2. Whisk together the caster sugar, double cream, flour and eggs.
3. Scatter the peach slices and raspberries across the base of the tart crust.
4. Pour the custard filling over the fruit and bake for 40 mins. Leave to cool completely before decorating.

Recommended crusts: plain pastry, almond, pistachio.

Chai Custard

60 MINS BAKED

INGREDIENTS

200ML MILK

200ML DOUBLE CREAM

3 EGGS

70G SUGAR

1 TSP CHAI SPICE MIX

METHOD

1. Preheat the oven to 160°/140° (fan)/ gas mark 3
2. In a medium saucepan, gently heat the milk, double cream and chai spice mix.
3. In a separate bowl, whisk together the eggs and sugar. Slowly pour the hot milk mixture into the eggs and sugar, whisking continuously.
4. Pour the custard into your tart case and bake for 40–45 mins. Leave to cool completely.

Recommended crusts: gingerbread, basic pastry, pistachio.

Dark Chocolate and Raspberry Swirl

2 HOURS CHILLED

INGREDIENTS

200G DARK CHOCOLATE, CHOPPED

200ML DOUBLE CREAM

50G RASPBERRY PURÉE

METHOD

1. Melt the chocolate in a heatproof bowl suspended over a pan of barely simmering water. Leave to cool and thicken for 5 mins.
2. Whip the cream until soft peaks form. Fold in the melted chocolate.
3. Spoon the chocolate cream into the tart case. Add the raspberry purée in blobs and use a toothpick to swirl it all together.
4. Chill for 2 hours or until fully set.

Recommended crusts: chocolate digestives, Oreo cookie, almond, chocolate cherry granola.

Rum and Raisin Cream

2 HOURS CHILLED

INGREDIENTS

200ML DOUBLE CREAM

150G CREAM CHEESE

2 TBSP RUM

50G RAISINS

METHOD

1. Whip the cream to soft peaks.
2. In a separate bowl, beat together the cream cheese and rum.
3. Gently fold the rum mixture into the whipped cream. Stir in the raisins.
4. Spoon the filling into the tart case and chill for 2 hours.

Recommended crusts: pistachio, basic biscuit, chocolate, walnut shortcrust.

Apricot Almond Cream

2 HOURS CHILLED

INGREDIENTS

200ML DOUBLE CREAM

150G CREAM CHEESE

50G APRICOT JAM

25G GROUND ALMONDS

METHOD

1. Whip the cream until soft peaks form.
2. In a separate bowl, beat together the cream cheese, apricot jam and ground almonds.
3. Gently fold the apricot cream mixture a third at a time, being careful not to knock too much air out of the whipped cream.
4. Spoon the filling into tart case and refrigerate for 2 hours.

Recommended crusts: almond, pistachio, cheat's carrot cake.

Mulled Wine Jelly

3 HOURS CHILLED

INGREDIENTS

250ML RED WINE

50G SUGAR

1 TSP CINNAMON

2 GELATINE LEAVES

METHOD

1. Heat the wine with the sugar and cinnamon.
2. Soften the gelatine in cold water. Squeeze out any excess water and whisk the gelatine into the wine.
3. Wrap foil or cling film around the base of your tart tin in case there are any leakages. Pour the jelly mixture into the crust and leave to set, preferably overnight.

Recommended crusts: gingerbread, basic pastry.

Black Forest

40 MINS BAKED

INGREDIENTS

220ML DOUBLE CREAM

100ML WHOLE MILK

260G DARK CHOCOLATE, CHOPPED

15G CASTER SUGAR

¼ TSP SALT

2 MEDIUM EGGS

80G MIXED BERRIES

METHOD

1. Preheat the oven to 160°/140° (fan)/ gas mark 3.
2. Whisk together the caster sugar, salt and eggs. Set aside.
3. Heat the milk and cream until close to boiling point. Remove the pan from the hob and stir in the chopped dark chocolate until completely melted.
4. Pour the hot chocolate mixture over the eggs and whisk until smooth.
5. Spoon the berries into the tart case and cover with the chocolate custard.
6. Bake for 20–25 mins or until slightly firm. Leave to cool completely before decorating.

Recommended crusts: chocolate pastry, plain pastry, almond (for a bit of a twist).

Salted Caramel

60 MINS BAKED

INGREDIENTS

400ML DOUBLE CREAM

112G CASTER SUGAR

6 MEDIUM EGG YOLKS

28G MUSCOVADO SUGAR

1 TSP SALT

METHOD

1. Preheat the oven to 100°/80° (fan)/gas mark 1.
2. Whisk together the egg yolks and muscovado sugar. Set aside.
3. Gently heat the caster sugar, resisting the temptation to stir. Give the pan a gentle shake from side to side if you must, but do not stir the sugar. It will crystalise and you will only regret it later.
4. While the sugar is on the hob, warm the cream in a separate pan.
5. Once the sugar has transformed into an amber-hued syrup, add the cream, whisking continuously. Be warned: this mixture will foam and hiss like nobody's business, so add the cream slowly and keep that whisk going.
6. Remove the caramel pan from the heat and stir in the egg mixture a little at a time.
7. Pour the caramel into the tart case and sprinkle with salt. Bake for 45–55 mins, or until the caramel is fairly set. Leave to cool and firm completely before decorating.

Coconut Lime Cream

2 HOURS CHILLED

INGREDIENTS

250ML DOUBLE CREAM

200G CREAM CHEESE

ZEST AND JUICE OF 2 LIMES

50G DESICCATED COCONUT

METHOD

1. Whip the cream until soft peaks form.
2. Beat the cream cheese with lime juice and zest.
3. Carefully fold the cream into the cream cheese mixture and stir in the desiccated coconut.
4. Spoon the filling into the tart case. Refrigerate for 2 hours.

Recommended crusts: coconut macaroon, almond, maple porridge oat.

Bourbon Chocolate Pudding

1.5 HOURS BAKED

INGREDIENTS

200G DARK CHOCOLATE

250ML DOUBLE CREAM

2 TBSP BOURBON

3 EGG YOLKS

25G CASTER SUGAR

METHOD

1. Preheat the oven to 160°/140° (fan)/gas mark 3.
2. Melt the chocolate in a heatproof bowl suspended over a pan of barely simmering water.
3. Stir in the cream and bourbon before moving the bowl away from the heat. Leave to cool slightly.
4. Whisk together the egg yolks and caster sugar. Carefully fold in the chocolate bourbon mixture.
5. Pour the filling into the tart case. Bake for 25–30 mins, or until the edges are set.

Recommended crusts: chocolate digestives, chocolate pastry, Oreo cookie.

Carrot Cake Spiced Cream Cheese

2 HOURS CHILLED

INGREDIENTS

200G CREAM CHEESE

250ML DOUBLE CREAM

80G ICING SUGAR

1 TSP CINNAMON

½ TSP GINGER

¼ TSP NUTMEG

METHOD

1. Whip the cream until soft peaks form.
2. Beat the cream cheese along with the icing sugar and spices.
3. Fold the whipped cream into the spiced cream cheese mixture.
4. Spoon the filling into the tart case, adding an extra flourish of nutmeg if you wish.
5. Chill for 2 hours, or until set.

Recommended crusts: cheat's carrot cake, basic biscuit, almond.

Tiramisu Tart

3 HOURS CHILLED

INGREDIENTS

250G MASCARPONE

150ML CREAM

3 TBSP COFFEE

2 TBSP MARSALA WINE

4 SPONGE FINGERS, SOAKED IN COFFEE

METHOD

1. Whip the cream to soft peaks.
2. Whisk together the mascarpone and Marsala.
3. Fold the two cream mixtures into one another.
4. Layer the coffee-soaked sponge fingers in the base of the tart case. Pour the cream mixture over the top.
5. Leave to chill for 3 hours.

Recommended crusts: basic biscuit, chocolate digestives.

Toasted Marshmallow S'mores

1 HOUR BAKED

INGREDIENTS

100G DARK CHOCOLATE, CHOPPED

150ML DOUBLE CREAM

100G MINI MARSHMALLOWS

METHOD

1. Whip the cream to soft peaks.
2. Melt the chocolate in a heatproof bowl suspended over a pan of barely simmering water. Remove the pan from the heat and leave the chocolate to cool for 5 mins.
3. Spoon the filling into the tart case. Top with the mini marshmallows and refrigerate for 2 hours.
4. Once set, use a culinary blowtorch to toast the marshmallows.

Recommended crusts: chocolate digestives, Oreo cookie, salted pretzel.

Hazelnut Mocha Custard

60 MINS BAKED

INGREDIENTS

200ML MILK

200ML DOUBLE CREAM

3 EGG YOLKS

100G CASTER SUGAR

1 TBSP COFFEE

2 TBSP HAZELNUT PASTE

METHOD

1. Preheat the oven to 160°/140° (fan)/gas mark 3.
2. In a medium saucepan, heat the milk, cream, coffee and hazelnut paste.
3. Whisk together the eggs and caster sugar. Pour a little of the milk mixture over the eggs, whisking continuously. Repeat with the rest of the mixture until well combined.
4. Bake for 35–40 mins. Leave to cool completely before removing the tart from the tin.

Recommended crusts: walnut shortcrust, chocolate digestives, churro doughnut, hazelnut pastry.

Pineapple and Coconut Panna Cotta

3 HOURS CHILLED

INGREDIENTS

200ML DOUBLE CREAM

200ML COCONUT MILK

2 GELATINE LEAVES

100G PINEAPPLE PURÉE

METHOD

1. Soften the gelatine in cold water.
2. Heat the cream and coconut milk until simmering. Stir in the gelatine (squeezing out any excess liquid first) and pineapple purée.
3. Remove the pan from the heat and leave to cool before pouring into your tart case. Refrigerate for 3 hours or until set.

Recommended crusts: coconut macaroon, basic biscuit, almond.

White Chocolate and Matcha Cream

2 HOURS   CHILLED

INGREDIENTS

200G WHITE CHOCOLATE

150ML DOUBLE CREAM

1 TSP MATCHA POWDER

150G MASCARPONE

METHOD

1. Melt the chocolate in a heatproof bowl suspended over a pan of barely simmering water. Leave to cool slightly once fully melted.
2. Whip the cream to soft peaks.
3. In a separate bowl, stir together the mascarpone, matcha powder and cooled white chocolate. Fold the matcha mixture into the whipped cream a little at a time.
4. Spoon the filling into the tart case. Leave to set for 2 hours.

Recommended crusts: almond, basic biscuit, pistachio.

The Designs

Tart it up

Now for the fun part: tarting it up. A difficulty rating is provided for each design, although we do have templates and all manner of sneaky tips to make even the most complex-looking tart as easy as pie. Don't stress over the details; the joy of sugar craft is letting your imagination run riot. Pink fox? No problem! Gingerbread village looking like it's been stomped on by Godzilla? Fine, tell everyone that's what you set out to do! This is about fun, not perfection.

COATINGS

Each tart is covered in 105g of sugar paste (also known as ready-to-roll icing/ fondant), or 200g icing sugar mixed with a little water. Personally, I prefer sugar paste for most of these projects, as it is more durable. If you prefer the latter method, please make sure the icing is well set before decorating.

MATERIALS

It is easier and cheaper to keep a small stock of food colourings rather than buying coloured sugar paste, which often goes hard before you get through it. Please, for the love of tart, do not waste your money on liquid colourings from supermarkets – they provide little depth of colour and can spoil icing. A tub of gel colour costs marginally more, lasts over a year, and will not ruin your icing/worktops/day.

USING THE TEMPLATES

You can find the templates in the last chapter of this book, on page 194. Trace the templates onto a sheet of baking /greaseproof paper. Imprint the image onto the sugar paste using a tracing wheel or sharp knife. Remove the paper before cutting out the shapes. *Voilà*, you're ready to decorate.

Fox in the Flowers

I've graded this foxy fellow as intermediate, but he certainly sits at the lower end of that scale. If you're not feeling particularly foxy today, leave him out and just scatter some fresh lavender across the top of the tart (as per the image on the inside cover of the back of this book).

A reminder about edible flowers. Make sure your lavender is from a plant away from traffic or where dog walkers tend to wander. If you cannot be certain if a plant has been chemically treated, find an edible flower site online and buy some there. Better to be safe.

INGREDIENTS

105G WHITE SUGAR PASTE

FOR THE FOX

20G ORANGE SUGAR PASTE

5G WHITE SUGAR PASTE

1G BLACK SUGAR PASTE

1 TBSP SUGAR PEARLS/SPRINKLES

FRESH LAVENDER

ICING SUGAR FOR DUSTING

METHOD

1. Sprinkle a thin layer of icing sugar over your worktop and roll out the white sugar paste. Using the tart tin base as a template, run a sharp knife or pizza cutter around the edge to create a 20cm circle.
2. Transfer the icing circle to the top of the tart, retaining the offcuts for later.
3. Using a sheet of greaseproof baking paper, trace the fox outline from the template chapter at the end of this book.
4. Roll out the orange sugar paste. Place the fox template on top and run a tracing wheel or knife around the edges. Remove the template and carefully cut out the fox shape.
5. Add the fox to the top of the tart using a paintbrush dipped in a little water. Use the same stencil to trace and cut out the detail pieces from the remaining white icing.

6. Use a little water to glue the white details to our foxy fellow. Roll two little eyes out of the black icing and top with a dab of white to make them sparkle. Use the remaining black icing to make his nose.
7. Scatter fresh lavender over the top of the tart, leaving space for the fox to peek out. If you don't have lavender to hand, fresh herbs will also look lovely.
8. Add a few sugar sprinkles to finish.

EASY

Summer Wreath

This is hands down one of my all-time favourite designs. It is simple. Takes a very short time to complete and always looks lovely. You can use any berries (I've even made it with chocolates instead of fruit) and mix and match as you please. If you've got an occasion coming up and are feeling particularly creative, you could write a message in the centre of the wreath using royal icing or a little edible lustre mixed with rejuvenator spirit or vodka (seriously).

INGREDIENTS

105G WHITE SUGAR PASTE

60G RASPBERRIES

50G BLUEBERRIES

60G STRAWBERRIES

FRESH MINT

MINT FLOWERS, IF IN SEASON

ICING SUGAR, FOR DUSTING

METHOD

1. Gently wash the fruit in a little water.
2. Slice the strawberries in half, leaving the stalks intact if you wish.
3. Sprinkle the worktop with a little icing sugar and roll out the white sugar paste. Place the base of the tart tin on top of the icing and run a sharp knife or pizza cutter around the edge. Place the icing circle on top of the tart.
4. Create a wreath by scattering the berries around the perimeter of the tart. Add a few fresh mint leaves and mint flowers (if in season) to finish.

Tip: For a boozy bonus, macerate the berries. The night before you are planning on decorating your tart, place the berries in a bowl and cover with 30g sugar and 60ml champagne, prosecco or brandy. Give the mixture a quick stir, cover and refrigerate overnight. Decorate the tart with the macerated berries, saving the remaining syrup to drizzle over each slice upon serving.

ne voyage de la
famille est agré

EASY

Watercolour Petals

Sometimes the simplest techniques produce the most stunning results. A dib-dib here and a dab-dab there, and *voilà*, a beautiful piece of tart art. I prefer to use powder colours for this, but gels work just as fine as long as you use them sparingly.

A note on flowers: although the watercolour images resemble hydrangeas, stick to rose petals for the decoration. Hydrangea flowers are not food-safe, so please keep them off.

INGREDIENTS

105G WHITE SUGAR PASTE

PINK, GREEN, DUSKY ROSE AND YELLOW FOOD COLOURING

REJUVENATOR SPIRIT/VODKA

EDIBLE PETALS OR SUGAR PETALS MADE FROM SUGAR PASTE TINTED WITH PINK FOOD COLOURING

METHOD

1. Roll out the white sugar paste. Place the base of the tart tin over the icing and run a sharp knife or pizza cutter around the edges. Pop the icing circle on top of the tart.
2. Mix a little dusky rose colouring with a dash of rejuvenator spirit or vodka to loosen. If you are using powder colours, add a little extra liquid to create a watercolour effect.
3. Take your paintbrush and dab clouds of colour across the lower sections of the tart, almost as though you are painting big, blousy bundles of hydrangeas.
4. Mix a little yellow colouring and dab away between the pink areas. Don't worry if you make any mistakes; you can cover any boo-boos with petals later.
5. Use the brighter pink to highlight the dusky rose areas. Dab towards the tops of the bundles, where the sunlight would naturally hit. Use the green to add some leaves.
6. Finish with a scattering of edible flower petals before serving.

INTERMEDIATE

Pup Tart

Two sausage dogs, wearing shades, and floating in a pool. I mean, what more could you want out of a tart?

We're using the template slightly differently this time, referring to it as a sizing reference rather than a stencil for cutting. I like to make everything on top of the stencil first, before transferring the decorations to the tart and adding sprinkles. You can also make the decorative pieces a few days ahead if you wish, just keep them on a sheet of greaseproof paper so they're easily transferable when it's time to serve up.

INGREDIENTS

105G BLUE SUGAR PASTE	5G PURPLE SUGAR PASTE
30G IVORY SUGAR PASTE	BLACK EDIBLE LUSTRE DUST
10G HOT PINK SUGAR PASTE	REJUVENATOR SPIRIT
1G PALE PINK SUGAR PASTE	30G MULTICOLOUR SPRINKLES

METHOD

1. Roll out the blue sugar paste. Place the base of the tart tin over the icing and cut around the edge with a sharp knife or pizza wheel. Pop the blue disc on top of the tart.
2. Trace around the pup tart template at the back of this book. Take the hot pink sugar paste and mould it into a rectangle, using the template as a size guide. Use the blunt side of a knife to create a few seams across the rectangle. Boom, now you have a pool float.
3. Take a portion of the ivory sugar paste and roll it into a cylinder the size and length of your first sausage dog. Stick the sausage to the pool float using a paintbrush dipped in water.
4. Using a little more ivory sugar paste, hand mould the head, paws, tail and ears of your pool-float pooch, sticking them together with water.

5. Repeat the two previous steps to create your second sausage dog. Pop him in the 'water' alongside his friend. Roll out the purple sugar paste into a tube and place it over the second dog to create his water donut.
6. Mix a small amount of black edible lustre dust with rejuvenator spirit and paint our pooch pals' noses, paws, sunglasses and cheeky grins. For a 3D effect, mould the sunglasses out of leftover ivory icing and paint them black.
7. Run a damp paintbrush around the perimeter of the tart and cover with sprinkles. If you have any star/fun-shaped sprinkles to hand, you can use some to decorate the pool donut.

INTERMEDIATE

Snow Stag

A winter favourite, this serene scene is incredibly easy to put together. I've used flower paste for the stag as it is tougher and sets much harder than regular sugar paste. However, if you happen to buy a 200g bar of chocolate instead of 150g, you can melt some of the leftover squares to create the stag instead. I personally prefer to use flower paste as it has a little stretch and is less brittle than chocolate, but just run with whatever you have to hand.

The mould for this tart can be found on Amazon for a couple of pounds, although be sure to check the sizes before ordering. The one I have used is 5cm tall.

INGREDIENTS

- 150G WHITE CHOCOLATE
- 35ML DOUBLE CREAM
- 5G WHITE FLOWER PASTE
- 6 SPRIGS FRESH ROSEMARY
- 1 TBSP SUGAR PEARLS/SPRINKLES
- 1 TBSP SNOWFLAKE SPRINKLES
- GOLD EDIBLE LUSTRE DUST
- EDIBLE SHIMMER DUST

METHOD

1. Take the fluffiest brush you own and dust the stag mould with gold edible lustre. Roll the flower paste between your palms to soften slightly. Press the paste into your stag mould, running a sharp knife over the back to remove any excess. Pop the mould in the freezer for at least an hour.
2. Roughly chop the white chocolate before transferring it to a large bowl. Heat the cream until it is just about to hit boiling point (small bubbles will be forming around the edges of the pan). Pour the hot cream over the chopped chocolate and leave to stand for 2 mins.
3. Fold the chocolate and cream together to create a smooth ganache. If the chocolate has failed to fully melt, place the bowl over a pan of barely simmering water, stirring continuously until smooth. Leave to cool.

4. Once the ganache has cooled enough to reach a spreadable texture (think margarine, fresh out of the fridge), spread a rough layer across the top of the tart. Refrigerate for 20 mins before adding a second, coarser layer across the bottom section of the tart.
5. Place the stag mould face down on a piece of greaseproof paper. Carefully peel the mould away to reveal the golden stag below.
6. Transfer the stag to the centre of the tart. Layer up the rosemary sprigs to create two fir trees before giving them a heavy dusting of edible shimmer powder. Add the sprinkles and snowflakes before finishing with a final flourish of shimmer.

EASY

Petals and Pistachio

Great news, friends, it's bonus recipe time: pistachio and rose may be a niche combination, but it would be absolutely criminal of me not to include one of my favourite recommendations in this book. Start with the pistachio crust, no amendments necessary. Next, jump to the chocolate caramel filling, but leave out the caramel and add a teaspoon of rose extract to the chocolate ganache before pouring it into the tart base. Leave to set before decorating as per this recipe. Beautiful.

INGREDIENTS

- 105G WHITE SUGAR PASTE
- 40G ICING SUGAR
- 10G UNSALTED BUTTER
- ½ TSP VANILLA EXTRACT
- 1 TSP MILK
- 5G EDIBLE DRIED FLOWERS
- 5G PISTACHIOS, SHELLED AND CHOPPED
- EXTRA ICING SUGAR, FOR DUSTING

METHOD

1. Make the buttercream by whisking together the icing sugar, unsalted butter, vanilla extract and milk. Set aside.
2. Sprinkle a little icing sugar over your worktop and roll out the white sugar paste. Using the tart tin base as a template, cut a 20cm circle out of the icing. Place the icing disc on top of the tart.
3. Load up a small palette knife (or the back of a spoon, if you don't have one) with buttercream. Press the buttercream onto the icing base and pull the implement away, slowly releasing the pressure as you go. This will create a loose petal/fan effect.
4. Repeat the previous step until you've no buttercream left. Sprinkle the edible petals and chopped pistachios over the buttercream detailing and serve.

EASY

Teddy-time Tart

If you go down to the woods today, you're sure of a big surprise ... A birthday favourite, my teddy-time tart is bright, fun and easy freakin' peasy. The shapes are pretty basic, meaning you may get away with not using the template if you can't be bothered cutting it out: a saucer and egg cup make excellent guides for the face and ears, a mug for his fluffy snout, with other pieces formed freehand.

INGREDIENTS

105G WHITE SUGAR PASTE

50G BROWN SUGAR PASTE

5G IVORY SUGAR PASTE

50G WHITE SUGAR PASTE TINTED PINK, ORANGE, BLUE AND PURPLE

1 TBSP SUGAR PEARLS/ SPRINKLES

A LITTLE ICING SUGAR, FOR DUSTING

METHOD

1. Roll out the white sugar paste on a lightly sugared worksurface. Place the base of your tart tin over the top and run a knife or pizza cutter around the edges. Pop the icing disc on top of your tart.
2. Trace the teddy bear template onto a sheet of baking/greaseproof paper. Roll out the brown icing and place the stencil over the top. Create an imprint of the bear by running a tracing wheel or sharp knife over the outline. Remove the stencil and cut out the teddy.
3. Repeat the previous step with the pink, white and black icings to create the rest of the teddy details.
4. Dip a paintbrush in water and use it to stick the ted to the bottom right side of the tart. Cut a selection of flowers out of different coloured icings and use them to frame our teddy friend. Dab the centre of each flower with water and add a sugar pearl to finish.

Tip: If you don't have any brown icing, cocoa powder kneaded into sugar paste works just as well.

INTERMEDIATE

Goodnight, Moon

This tart includes a peculiar (yet simple) technique for edible tissue (wafer paper). Sure, you could make the clouds from sugar paste, but they would lack the airy, ethereal quality of the tissue. I use the same material on wedding and celebration cakes as it makes a beautiful filler between flowers and sugar decorations. I once had someone ask if they could use prawn crackers instead. No. Please, don't do that. Just, no.

INGREDIENTS

105G NAVY SUGAR PASTE

40G WHITE SUGAR PASTE

1 SHEET EDIBLE WAFER PAPER

GOLD FOOD COLOURING

A LITTLE ICING SUGAR, FOR DUSTING

METHOD

1. Sprinkle a thin layer of icing sugar over your worktop and roll out the navy sugar paste. Using the tart tin base as a template, run a sharp knife or pizza cutter around the edge to create a 20cm circle.
2. Transfer the icing circle to the top of the tart.
3. Trace the moon template onto a sheet of greaseproof/baking paper. Imprint the moon motif into the white icing by placing the stencil on top and running a knife or tracing wheel over the outline.
4. Use a damp paintbrush to stick the moon to the tart. Cut out some sugar stars and add them to the tart before painting the details with the gold food colouring.
5. Tear up the wafer paper and blitz it in a blender with 100ml water.
6. Place a dry frying pan over a medium heat. Add a tablespoon of paper mixture and cook for one minute, or until the water has evaporated and you're left with edible tissue paper. Repeat with the remaining mixture one tablespoon at a time.
7. Tear the edible tissue into pieces and place on top of the tart to create your ethereal, edible clouds.

INTERMEDIATE

Winter Village

The quickest and easiest way to achieve this design is to make the gingerbread tart base with the chocolate filling, and use the dough offcuts for the village. However, I am leaving nothing to chance here: for all I know, you may have gone completely rogue and be crafting this design on a peachberry custard filling in a pistachio base. I've no idea how wild you people are. As such, in the interest of you rebels out there, I am starting this recipe from scratch.

I have used a mould by Karen Davies for this design (details can be found in the supplier list at the end of this book), but you can cut out your own village by hand if you prefer.

INGREDIENTS

150G DARK CHOCOLATE
200ML DOUBLE CREAM
40G UNSALTED BUTTER
33G DARK BROWN SUGAR
1.5 TBSP GOLDEN SYRUP
100G PLAIN FLOUR
½ TSP BICARBONATE OF SODA
1 TSP GROUND GINGER
80G ICING SUGAR
1 TBSP GOLD STAR SPRINKLES

METHOD

1. Preheat the oven to 200°/180°C (fan)/gas mark 6.
2. Melt the butter, dark brown sugar and golden syrup in a pan over a medium heat. Remove the pan from the hob and stir in the flour, bicarbonate of soda and ginger. Give the dough a quick knead to bring it together fully.
3. Press the dough into the crevices of the winter village mould, or roll it out onto a sheet of baking paper and cut out your decorations by hand. Refrigerate for 30 mins.
4. Bake the gingerbread for 10 mins. Leave to cool completely on a wire rack.

5. Chop the dark chocolate and transfer it to a large bowl. Heat the double cream until it just about hits boiling point. Pour the hot cream over the chocolate and leave it to settle in the pan for 2 mins before stirring. If the chocolate has not fully melted, place the bowl over a pan of barely simmering water and stir continuously until you have a smooth, creamy ganache. Leave to cool for 1 hour.
6. Spread the ganache over the top of the tart. Gently place a sheet of baking paper over two-thirds of the tart, giving the exposed third a generous dusting of icing sugar. Remove the paper and arrange the gingerbread village on top of the tart.
7. Finish by adding a scattering of gold stars and a light sprinkling of sugar snow across the sky and rooftops.

EASY

Fluttering Fans

I love this effect because (a) it looks *fancy*, and (b), it is so much easier than it looks. You will need a 5cm (2in) circular punch, but if you are in a bit of a jam, you can always draw around a beaker and cut the circles out with scissors. Alternatively, you could alter the design by cutting the paper into squares. There are no rules here, just follow your creative instinct and experiment.

INGREDIENTS

105G WHITE SUGAR PASTE

5 A4 SHEETS OF EDIBLE WAFER PAPER

1 TBSP WHITE SPRINKLES

A LITTLE ICING SUGAR, FOR DUSTING

METHOD

1. Dust your worktop with icing sugar and roll out the white sugar paste. Pop the tart tin on top of the icing and run a knife or pizza cutter around the edge. Transfer the icing disc to the top of the tart.
2. Using your paper punch or scissors, cut as many discs as possible out of the wafer paper sheets.
3. Tear up the remnants from the wafer paper sheets. Pop them in a bowl with 50ml water to create a thick, gloopy glue.
4. Take a paper disc and paint a stripe of glue down the centre. Top with a second disc and repeat four more times. Run one last stripe of glue down the centre of the top disc and fold the bundle in half to create a semicircular, fluffy fan.
5. Repeat with the remaining paper discs until you have several paper fans.
6. Attach the fans to the tart by brushing the underside seam with a little water. I like to bundle them up at jaunty angles, but feel free to run with whatever looks good to you.
7. Finish by adding a few sugar sprinkles to the blank side of the tart.

INTERMEDIATE

Up and Away

Oh, to be swept away by a bunch of balloons into a candy floss sky ... I have no doubt this little chap will float into a safe landing on a squidgy soft sugar cloud once he has finished his adventures. If you can't get hold of candyfloss, you can find jars of marshmallow fluff at most supermarkets, often wedged between the jars of jam and chocolate spreads. It is not as airy as candyfloss, but it is just as ethereal if you spoon it on carefully.

INGREDIENTS

105G WHITE SUGAR PASTE

20G CARAMEL SUGAR PASTE

5G PINK SUGAR PASTE

1G BLACK SUGAR PASTE

1G WHITE SUGAR PASTE (IN ADDITION TO THE 105G FOR THE BASE)

10G CANDYFLOSS

BLUE FOOD COLOURING

REJUVENATOR SPIRIT

20G GRAPES HALVED

A LITTLE ICING SUGAR, FOR DUSTING

METHOD

1. Dust your worktop with icing sugar and roll out the white sugar paste. Using the tart tin base as a guide, cut out a 20cm icing circle and place it on top of your tart.
2. Mix a dash of blue food colouring with a teaspoon of rejuvenator spirit/ clear alcohol. Using a fluffy paintbrush or clean sponge, dab the top of the tart with the blue colouring.
3. Trace the mouse from the template chapter onto greaseproof/baking paper. Roll out the caramel sugar paste and place the template on top. Use a tracing wheel or small knife to emboss the image before removing the template and cutting around the outline with a sharp knife.
4. Roll out the pink sugar paste. Use the same template to cut out the pieces for our mouse friend's tummy, nose and other pink details. Stick the pieces to the caramel outline using a damp paintbrush.

5. Use the black and remaining white icing to hand-mould the eyes, eyebrows and cheeky grin. Use the pink and white offcuts to roll out a tail and balloon strings.
6. Starting from the top and working your way down, stack the sliced grapes (cut side down) to create a balloon formation.
7. Finish by tearing the candy floss into clouds and dotting it around the tart. Up and away!

EASY

Rosemary Wreath

An incredibly swift and simple decorating job, I like to make this tart using the gingerbread base and dark chocolate and caramel filling. You can switch out the rosemary for thyme if you wish, or even use a combination of the two. If you catch them in season, fresh cranberries rolled in coarse sugar make a stunning addition or alternative to the pomegranate seeds.

INGREDIENTS

105G WHITE SUGAR PASTE

30G FRESH ROSEMARY

20G POMEGRANATE SEEDS

20G GOLD SPRINKLES

A LITTLE ICING SUGAR, FOR DUSTING

60CM RED RIBBON

METHOD

1. Sprinkle a thin layer of icing sugar over your worktop and roll out the white sugar paste. Using the tart tin base as a guide, run a sharp knife or pizza cutter around the edge to create a 20cm circle. Pop the icing circle on top of the tart.
2. Go through your sprigs of rosemary, picking out any pieces that have a natural curve. We want to save these 'hero' pieces for the top layer of the wreath.
3. Arrange the other pieces of rosemary around the edges of the tart. Place the hero pieces on top to create a smooth, curved finish.
4. Scatter the pomegranate seeds and sprinkles over the rosemary like Christmas baubles. Tie the ribbon into a bow and place it at the bottom of the wreath to finish.

Queen Cottontail

This doe-eyed cutie has been crowned with a flurry of fresh flowers (gosh, try saying that in a hurry). If you're feeling particularly creative, then you could go ahead and make sugar flowers, but edible blooms are just as beautiful and will finish your tart in a fraction of the time.

INGREDIENTS

105G WHITE SUGAR PASTE

65G GREY SUGAR PASTE

5G BLACK SUGAR PASTE

5G GREEN SUGAR PASTE

10G PINK SUGAR PASTE

EDIBLE FLOWERS/PETALS

A LITTLE ICING SUGAR, FOR DUSTING

METHOD

1. Dust your worktop with icing sugar and roll out the white sugar paste. Cut out a 20cm circle, using the tart tin base as a guide. Place the icing circle on top of your chosen tart.
2. Using greaseproof/baking paper, trace the bunny from the template chapter.
3. Roll out the grey sugar paste and place the template on top. Trace the pattern into the icing by running a tracing wheel or knife around the outline. Remove the stencil and cut out fully.
4. Stick the grey bunny base to the tart using a little water. Roll out the black, pink, green and remaining white icing. Use the template to cut out a little bunny nose, eyes and ears. Add the detail pieces to the grey bunny base, using a damp paintbrush to secure everything in place.
5. Run the paintbrush over the bunny's forehead. Create a flower crown using edible flowers and petals. Enjoy.

Tip: If you don't have access to edible flowers (or they are simply out of season), you can pull a 'Carmen Miranda' and create a crown of fresh fruit instead. Daintier fruits such as redcurrants and blueberries would look beautiful on a bed of strawberry slices and fresh mint leaves.

EASY

Playing Dress-up

A rose-scented ballgown, golden confetti and swags of sugared redcurrant balloons. What more could a gal want?

This is one of those rare occasions where I recommend coating the tart with an icing sugar and water mix rather than sugar-paste icing. It is so much easier to stick the petals to a slightly tacky icing top rather than faff about with edible glue and whatnot. It also helps to separate your petals by size before icing the tart, meaning you can put the skirt together swiftly before the surface sets completely.

INGREDIENTS

200G ICING SUGAR

1 SHEET EDIBLE WAFER PAPER

BLACK FOOD COLOURING

2 STALKS REDCURRANTS

1G BLACK SUGAR PASTE

PETALS FROM ONE LARGE RED ROSE

EDIBLE LUSTRE SPRAY

GOLD AND WHITE SPRINKLES

1 TBSP CASTER SUGAR

METHOD

1. Dampen the redcurrants with a little water and sprinkle with caster sugar. Set aside.
2. Take a piece of baking/greaseproof paper and trace the lady from the template chapter. Place your sheet of wafer paper over the template and use the black food colouring to paint the design. Leave to dry completely before carefully cutting out.
3. Mix the icing sugar with 3 tbsp water, stirring it in a spoonful at a time until you have a smooth, spreadable icing. Feel free to add more water if necessary.
4. Pour the icing over the tart and smooth it out with a palette knife or the back of a spoon.

5. When the icing has almost set, gently place the wafer paper lady on top of the tart.
6. Place one small petal over the top of the dress to create the bodice. Then, starting from the bottom and working your way up, layer the petals into a big, fluffy skirt. Roll a belt out of black sugar paste and place it over her waistline.
7. Scatter gold and white sprinkles like confetti falling over our starlet. Add the sugared redcurrants and spray with edible lustre to finish.

J'adore Paris

OK, we are all knew there was going to be a toughie somewhere within these pages. In all fairness, as long as you stay calm while piping, it isn't that difficult. If you're new to royal icing, I'd strongly recommend having a practice first. Using a plate or sheet of greaseproof paper, practise piping straight lines by pressing the nozzle to the surface and applying a gentle pressure to the bag, slowly releasing as you pull the nozzle away. If your nozzle gets clogged, take a pin or skewer and give it a good wiggle to break down what is most likely to be a lump of sugar. Practice does indeed make perfect, so take your time and be patient. You'll be *très magnifique* in two shakes of a croissant.

INGREDIENTS

200G ICING SUGAR

BLUE FOOD COLOURING

GOLD FOOD COLOURING

PINK EDIBLE PETALS

200G STORE-BOUGHT ROYAL ICING

OR

200G ICING SUGAR

1 EGG WHITE

1TSP LEMON JUICE

METHOD

1. If you're making your own royal icing, whisk the egg until thick, white and fluffy. Fold in 200g icing sugar and the teaspoon of lemon juice, stirring until smooth. Transfer the royal icing to a piping bag fitted with a no. 2 tip. If you don't have a piping nozzle, you can simply snip a 1mm piece off the end of the piping bag.
2. Whisk together the remaining 200g icing sugar and blue food colouring with 3–4 tbsp of water. Spread the blue icing over the top of the tart, using the back of a spoon to smooth it over.
3. Trace the Eiffel Tower motif onto a sheet of greaseproof paper. Flip the paper over, so the ink is on the underside. Take your royal icing bag and carefully pipe over the design. Leave to dry completely (preferably overnight).

4. There are two ways you can transfer your Eiffel Tower to your tart: the brave may gently slide a palette knife underneath and lift it from the paper. Personally, I like to flip the paper onto the tart itself and carefully peel away the backing.
5. Use an extra-fine paintbrush to gild the Eiffel Tower with gold food colouring. Use some of the leftover royal icing to pipe some fluffy clouds across the sky.
6. Pipe a zigzag of royal icing around the lower perimeter of the tart, working its way up to the left-hand side. Cover with edible flower petals and serve.

EASY

Bumble Tumble

This sugar sweet design is a great one for little hands as it requires no special tools or heat. You can use any edible flowers, just make sure they haven't been chemically treated or grown on roadsides (pollution or exhaust fumes do not a delicious flower make). It can be tempting to pick up a tray or pansies from the garden centre, but please do not do this unless you can be absolutely certain that they haven't been treated with any chemical nasties. Home-grown or those bought from edible flower specialists are safest and best.

INGREDIENTS

105G WHITE SUGAR PASTE

15G YELLOW SUGAR PASTE

10G BLACK SUGAR PASTE

15G FRESH THYME

FRESH EDIBLE FLOWERS (PANSIES OR VIOLAS ARE IDEAL)

A LITTLE ICING SUGAR, FOR DUSTING

METHOD

1. Sprinkle a thin layer of icing sugar over your worktop and roll out the white sugar paste. Using the tart tin as a template, run a sharp knife or pizza cutter around the edge to create a 20cm circle. Carefully transfer the icing disc to the top of the tart.
2. Divide the yellow sugar paste into three 5g portions. Roll each piece into an egg shape.
3. Using a paintbrush dipped in water, stick the three 'bumble bodies' to the surface of your tart.
4. Roll out the black sugar paste and cut out six stripes, each one approximately 5mm by 15mm long. Divide the remaining black sugar paste into three and roll each piece into a ball. Use a damp paintbrush to stick the stripes and noggins onto the bees.
5. Use some of the white sugar paste offcuts to mould six teardrop-shaped pieces. Moisten the backs of the bees and carefully add the wings.
6. Disperse the thyme sprigs across the lower section of the tart. Add the edible flowers and serve.

INTERMEDIATE

Chalkboard

Although it is generally fine to flip between gel and powder colours for these projects, this is the one tart where I'd really recommend sticking with an edible lustre dust for that messy, chalky effect. If you only have gel/liquid colours, you can create a similar effect by dusting a little icing sugar around the edges of the tart before painting.

The beauty of this design is that you can paint any message you wish. There are plenty of free font-generator websites that will transform your chosen sentiment into the style you're after. Just print it off and trace over it as you would with the templates in this book. Birthdays, congratulations, resignations, confessing a crime to the police – this tart can be used to convey a multitude of messages.

INGREDIENTS

105G BLACK SUGAR PASTE

WHITE EDIBLE LUSTRE DUST

REJUVENATOR SPIRIT/VODKA

A LITTLE ICING SUGAR, FOR DUSTING

METHOD

1. Sprinkle a thin layer of icing sugar over your worktop and roll out the black sugar paste. Using the tart tin base as a template, run a sharp knife or pizza cutter around the edges to create a 20cm circle. Pop the black disc on top of your tart.
2. Using a sheet of baking/greaseproof paper, trace over the chalkboard from the template chapter.
3. Place the template over the tart. Gently emboss the text into the icing using a tracing wheel or knife.
4. Take a small amount of white edible lustre dust and mix with a drop or rejuvenator spirit or clear alcohol. Use a fine paintbrush to carefully paint over the embossed design.
5. When the paint has dried, dust a small amount of white edible lustre around the edges of the tart to finish.

Tip: You can paint the black icing disc before placing it on the tart if you wish. This can be particularly helpful if you have shaky hands or sore wrists.

EASY

Blush Sails

Do spring roll wrappers (rice paper circles) belong on a dessert? Actually, they do. Dipped in tinted water and left to dry out overnight, this basic ingredient transforms into something undeniably pretty. You can soak the wrappers in any colour you wish, although they do look particularly wintery left untinted. Just use plain, lukewarm water and give them a good dusting with edible shimmer when dry.

INGREDIENTS

105G WHITE SUGAR PASTE

3 VIETNAMESE RICE PAPER CIRCLES

GOLD FOOD COLOURING

PINK FOOD COLOURING

EDIBLE SHIMMER DUST

A LITTLE ICING SUGAR, FOR DUSTING

METHOD

1. Carefully cut the rice paper circles into eighths. You will almost certainly have a few snap along the way, but don't panic – I considered breakage when calculating ingredient quantities.
2. Take a sheet of greaseproof/baking paper. Give it a good scrunch as you lay it out on the worktop.
3. Stir a couple of drops of pink food colouring into a bowl of lukewarm water. Drop a piece of rice paper into the bowl and leave it to soften for 1 min.
4. Carefully remove the rice paper from the bowl and lay it over the crumpled baking paper. Repeat with the remaining rice paper pieces and leave to dry overnight.
5. Dust your worktop with a little icing sugar and roll out the white sugar paste. Using the tart tin base as a template, cut out a disc of icing and pop it on top of the tart.
6. Load a paintbrush with gold food colouring and flick it over the tart.
7. Scatter the pink sails across one side of the tart, gilding the edges with a little gold food colouring. Spray with edible shimmer dust and serve.

Beehive Bedlam

How could you not love this little busy bee? Keep her happy with oodles of chocolate, honeycomb and creamy fudge pieces (although chocolate chips, crushed nuts or, dare I say it, crystallised ginger, would work just as well). If you're struggling to get your hands on golden blonde chocolate, white chocolate will do. Just give it an extra brush of gold edible lustre dust when it's done setting.

INGREDIENTS

105G WHITE SUGAR PASTE

60G GOLDEN BLONDE CHOCOLATE

15G FUDGE CUBES

10G MARZIPAN

2G BLACK SUGAR PASTE

GOLD EDIBLE LUSTRE DUST

A LITTLE ICING SUGAR, FOR DUSTING

METHOD

1. Break the golden blonde chocolate into small pieces. You can either melt it in short bursts in the microwave (giving the chocolate a good stir every 20 seconds) or in a heatproof bowl placed over a pan of barely simmering water.
2. Pour the melted chocolate over a clean sheet of bubble wrap. Using a palette knife, gently work the chocolate into the crevices between the bubbles. Leave to set completely.
3. Dust the worktop with icing sugar and roll out the white sugar paste. Using the tart tin base as a guide, cut out a 20cm round disc of icing and pop it on top of your tart.
4. Peel the bubble wrap away from the chocolate and break it into small shards. Dust the honeycomb with a little gold edible lustre dust.
5. Scatter the honeycomb pieces across the lower part of the tart. Roll the marzipan into a cylinder, tapering off one end. Use the black and white sugar pastes to create the stripes, eyes, legs and other honeybee details. Give her a little smile using the end of a teaspoon and stick her to the tart using a damp paintbrush.

6. Finish by dampening the edges of the tart and decorating with fudge pieces. Give your honeybee a cube of fudge for her hard work, and serve.

EASY

Citrus Meringue

OK, we're cheating *just* a little here by using store-bought meringue nests. If you're the kind of crazy cat who prefers to go *au naturel*, you can whisk two large egg whites to stiff peaks before adding 1 tsp cornflour and 110g caster sugar, whisking as you go. Scoop the meringue onto a tray lined with baking paper and pop it in the oven for 30 mins at 150°/130° (fan)/gas mark 2. Or you could just throw some pre-baked meringues in your supermarket trolley. The power is in your hands.

INGREDIENTS

1 LEMON

1 LIME

1 ORANGE

30G MERINGUE NESTS

METHOD

1. Preheat the oven on its lowest setting. Line a tray with baking paper in preparation.
2. Slice the lemon, lime and orange into 2–5mm thick rounds (a mandoline, if you have one, will make this much easier). Transfer the slices to the baking paper, spreading them out in a single layer. Bake in the oven for 1 hour, flipping the slices over at the halfway point. Leave to cool completely on a wire rack.
3. Arrange the dried citrus slices around the edge of your tart. Crumble the meringue nests into the centre before giving them a quick blast with a culinary blowtorch.

Tip: The torching of the meringues is for aesthetics only (they are already cooked and fully dried out). As such, you can leave the meringues plain if you don't have a culinary blowtorch to hand. Leave the Black & Decker in the shed.

INTERMEDIATE

Rainbow Road

This little guy can slide down his rainbow and into my direct messages any time. Feel free to go crazy with colour here, adding sprinkles, stars, edible glitter, whatever you fancy. He's a unicorn, he was made to be 'extra'.

INGREDIENTS

105G WHITE SUGAR PASTE

20G UNSALTED BUTTER

80G ICING SUGAR

10G CANDY FLOSS

GOLD, BLACK, PINK, PURPLE, YELLOW, BLUE, GREEN AND RED FOOD COLOURING

A LITTLE ICING SUGAR, FOR DUSTING

METHOD

1. Sprinkle a thin layer of icing sugar over your worktop and roll out the white sugar paste. Using the tart tin base as a template, run a sharp knife or pizza cutter around the edges to create a 20cm circle for the top of your tart.
2. Whisk together the butter and icing sugar, adding a splash of milk if it feels a little thick. Divide the frosting between six small bowls or egg cups, and tint with the rainbow colours.
3. Heap a spoonful of each colour at the base of the tart. Take a palette knife and spread the frosting in one swift swoosh. If it looks a bit wibbly, that's the point: we want it to fade out as it goes.
4. Trace the unicorn template onto a sheet of baking/greaseproof paper. Roll out the remaining white sugar paste and place the template on top. Using a tracing wheel or knife, emboss the outline into the icing. Cut out the unicorn shape and place him on the rainbow. Use the same template to cut out the hooves and unicorn horn. Stick the detail pieces to the unicorn using a damp paintbrush.
5. Paint the hooves and horn gold before carefully adding the facial detail with black paint.
6. Cut out some sugar paste stars and paint them gold. Tint a little sugar paste pink and roll it into thin pieces to create the hair. Finally, add some candy floss clouds at the end of the rainbow to finish.

ADVANCED

Smooth Sailing

This may look complicated, but trust me, you can do this! It is more about the cutting out than anything else. Just take your time and consider holding your wrist with your free hand when painting, it does wonders for keeping your brush steady and your mind clear.

INGREDIENTS

105G NAVY SUGAR PASTE

50G WHITE SUGAR PASTE

10G BROWN SUGAR PASTE

20G CARAMEL SUGAR PASTE

50G UNSALTED BUTTER

100G ICING SUGAR

BLUE, GOLD, BLACK AND BROWN FOOD COLOURING

5G ROYAL ICING

ICING SUGAR, FOR DUSTING

METHOD

1. Sprinkle a thin layer of icing sugar over your worktop and roll out the navy sugar paste. Using the tart tin as a template, run a sharp knife or pizza cutter around the edge to make a 20cm circle for the top of your tart. Splatter with gold food colouring.
2. Take a portion of white sugar paste and roll it into two long pieces approximately 3mm wide. Wrap the two pieces around one another to create a rope (although you are welcome to use a rope mould if you wish). Repeat until you have enough rope to frame the tart. Stick the pieces down with a dab of water before painting them gold.
3. Whisk together the butter, icing sugar and a dash of blue food colouring. Add a splash of milk if the frosting feels a little thick. Spread the frosting roughly across the bottom half of the tart, saving a little for later.
4. Trace the template onto baking/greaseproof paper. Roll out the brown and caramel sugar pastes and emboss the motif into the icing using a tracing wheel or knife. Carefully cut the pieces out and arrange on the tart. Cover the base of the boat with the leftover blue frosting.

5. Use the black food colouring to paint the details on the ship, sails and banner. Dab some watered-down brown food colouring around the edges of the sails and motto for a weathered effect.
6. Pipe zigzags of royal icing along the edges of the waves. Dip a paintbrush in water and drag the royal icing away to create sugar seafoam.
7. Finally mould the anchor out of the remaining white sugar paste. Paint it gold and add it to the bottom left of the tart.

INTERMEDIATE

Retro Ink

You can use pre-coloured sugar paste for this design if you wish, but the colours are used in such small quantities that I find it more cost effective to tint my own. If you do decide to buy coloured sugar paste, you can make it last a lot longer by keeping it tightly wrapped in tinfoil. Dried or crusted sugar paste can be revived by trimming away the hard edges and kneading in a little vegetable shortening (such as Trex) until smooth. Nothing goes to waste on my watch.

INGREDIENTS

140G WHITE SUGAR PASTE

PINK, RED, BLUE, BLACK, PURPLE, ORANGE, YELLOW AND GREEN FOOD COLOURING

A LITTLE ICING SUGAR, FOR DUSTING

METHOD

1. Coat the top of your tart with a 20cm round disc of white sugar paste. Roll out your icing and use the base of the tart tin as a template.
2. Divide the remaining icing into seven evenly sized portions. Use a few drops of each food colour to create pink, red, blue, yellow, purple, orange and green sugar pastes.
3. Trace the retro ink template onto a sheet of greaseproof/baking paper.
4. Dust your worktop with icing sugar and roll out each of the sugar paste colours. Use a tracing wheel or sharp knife to emboss each of the tattoo details into their respective sugar pastes. Remove the template and carefully cut the details out of the icing.
5. Moisten the top of the tart with a damp paintbrush. Gently transfer the icing pieces, using the template as a placement guide.
6. Dip a fine paintbrush into the black food colouring and paint the outlines around each of the tattoos. Don't worry if it's a little wobbly, it's meant to look a bit retro.
7. Finish by adding some black speckles to each of the motifs.

INTERMEDIATE

Pretty Porcelain

This Wedgwood-esque tart is created using nothing but royal icing, water and a paintbrush. There are two reasons why I haven't created a template for this: firstly, because I'm not the sort of sociopath to encourage you to pipe royal icing over a sheet of carefully defined lines. You will hate both me and this book in equal measure. Secondly, because the wobblier the pattern is, the better the overall result. You may not believe it now, but freehand is certainly the more sensible option in this scenario.

INGREDIENTS

105G BLUE SUGAR PASTE

1 MEDIUM EGG WHITE

200G ICING SUGAR

1 TBSP LEMON JUICE

EXTRA ICING SUGAR, FOR DUSTING

METHOD

1. Whisk the egg white until fluffy and foamy. Fold in the icing sugar and lemon juice before transferring the royal icing to a piping bag.
2. Roll out the blue sugar paste on a lightly sugared worktop. Cut out a 20cm circle of icing and pop it on top of your tart.
3. Snip the end off the piping bag. Pipe out a rough flower – the wobblier the better. Dip a paintbrush in water and use it to drag the outer edges of the flower inwards. Add another four wobbly petals and repeat.
4. Continue the pattern across the tart as per the guide images. If you prefer a maximalist design, you can fill the negative space with leaves, swirls and dots. Continue to pipe and spread until you are happy with the final overall tart art.

EASY

Rainbow Fish

This bright, jolly fellow can be dressed up in any assortment of colours (he is a rainbow fish, after all). If you have the extra mixing and washing-up time, he would look particularly snazzy in five or six colours with a sprinkling of edible glitter, should you be so bold. If you are not a fan of food colouring, natural tints such as butterfly pea powder, dried beetroot, matcha and turmeric powder produce an equally delightful result.

INGREDIENTS

60G WHITE SUGAR PASTE

200G ICING SUGAR

50G UNSALTED BUTTER

1 TSP VANILLA EXTRACT

2 TBSP MILK

2G BLACK SUGAR PASTE

3 FOOD COLOURINGS OF YOUR CHOICE

METHOD

1. Divide the white sugar paste into four 15g portions. Use two to make the upper and lower fins, one to make a tail and the final piece to make the lips, eye and side fin.
2. Moisten the tail with a damp paintbrush and stick it to the tart. Repeat with upper and lower fins and mouthpiece.
3. Whisk together the icing sugar, butter, vanilla extract and milk to make the buttercream. Divide the buttercream between three bowls and tint each one with a dab of food colouring.
4. Using a palette knife or back of a teaspoon, coat each of the icing details (such as the fins) with buttercream.
5. Transfer the frostings into three piping bags. Snip a 2cm wide opening in the end of each bag. Pipe alternating coloured blobs of buttercream down one side of the fish. Press a teaspoon into each blob and swoosh away. Pipe another row and repeat until the tart is fully covered.
6. Press the eye into the buttercream, adding a small circle of black sugar paste for the pupil.
7. Add the side fin and cover with frosting to finish.

EASY

Buttercream Flowers

The beauty of this design is that there are no specialist piping techniques involved. Sure, there are plenty of incredible buttercream flower techniques out there, but let's keep it simple for once. Each flower is created by layering up dots of buttercream – that's it. You could even get away with not using the star nozzle if you don't mind a slightly different look, just layer up those buttercream blobs for a fluffy floral effect.

INGREDIENTS

105G WHITE SUGAR PASTE

25G UNSALTED BUTTER

100G ICING SUGAR

PINK, LAVENDER AND GREEN FOOD COLOURING

EXTRA ICING SUGAR, FOR DUSTING

EDIBLE SHIMMER SPRAY

1 TSP SUGAR PEARLS

METHOD

1. Sprinkle a thin layer of icing sugar over your worktop and roll out the white sugar paste. Using the tart tin base as a template, run a sharp knife or pizza cutter around the edge to create a 20cm circle. Place the icing circle on top of the tart.
2. Whisk together the butter and icing sugar to create a stiff buttercream. If it feels a little dry, add a tablespoon of milk to loosen.
3. Divide the buttercream between four bowls. It may not look like much, but we only need a small amount of each colour for this design. Tint three of the bowls with food colouring, leaving the last one plain.
4. Transfer the plain buttercream to a piping bag fitted with a small star nozzle. Transfer the colour frostings to three separate piping bags fitted with no. 2 size nozzles, or with no nozzles and the end snipped off.
5. Pipe several random stalks of green frosting across the lower half of the tart. Add some leaves by piping a dot of buttercream and continuing to squeeze the bag as you pull it away.

6. Starting at the top of one of your stalks, pipe a series of lavender dots in a cone shape, tapering off like a head of lavender. Next, take the pink buttercream and pipe five small dots in a circular formation. Pop a pearl in the centre to create a flower.
7. Finally, take the plain buttercream and pipe a cloud of frosting stars at the tops of your longest stalks. Use any leftover pink and lavender buttercream to add a scattering of polka dots across the canvas. Finish with a spritz of edible lustre spray.

EASY

Ombre Wave

This uncomplicated design is perfect for a peaceful afternoon's baking. I've opted for pinks here, but these ombre waves will look beautiful in any shade. If you have a little more time (and patience) on your hands, this would look particularly lovely in rainbow hues, flowing from red to blue.

INGREDIENTS

200G WHITE SUGAR PASTE

FOOD COLOURING OF YOUR CHOICE

1 TBSP SUGAR PEARLS/SPRINKLES

A LITTLE ICING SUGAR, FOR DUSTING

METHOD

1. Dust your worktop with icing sugar and roll out 100g of the white sugar paste. Cut out a 20cm wide circle (using your tart tin as a guide) and place it on top of your tart.
2. Divide the remaining icing into five pieces. Use your chosen food colouring to tint four of the sugar paste portions, getting slightly darker as you go.
3. Roll our your five shades of sugar paste. Use a pizza cutter to cut them into wobbly strips approximately 2cm wide.
4. Brush the top of the tart with a little water. Starting with the white pieces, later the strips from light to dark, trimming the edges as you go.
5. Add a few sugar sprinkles to finish.

INTERMEDIATE

Wilf the Dog

Just look at that little face! I've created an easy to follow photo guide to make this little chap as simple as possible. For a chocolatey terrier option, add 2 tbsp cocoa to the buttercream while mixing.

INGREDIENTS

- 50G UNSALTED BUTTER
- 200G ICING SUGAR
- 1 TSP VANILLA EXTRACT
- 2 TBSP MILK
- 10G BLACK SUGAR PASTE
- 2G PINK SUGAR PASTE
- 1G WHITE SUGAR PASTE

METHOD

1. Whisk together the icing sugar, butter, vanilla extract and milk, to create a smooth buttercream. Spoon the frosting into a piping bag fitted with a large star nozzle.
2. Using the photo guide, start by piping the ears, followed by the forehead. Pipe his fluffy chin and the upper part of his face, followed by his magnificently moustachioed snout.
3. Roll two eyes and a nose out of the black sugar paste. Hand-mould the pink sugar paste into a teardrop shape before pressing the blunt side of a knife down the centre to create a tongue.
4. Carefully arrange the eyes, nose and tongue on our furry friend's face. Dab the eyes with a damp paintbrush and add a dot of white sugar paste to bring them to life.
5. Finish by piping two thick buttercream eyebrows. What a handsome boy.

Pinkie Pie

I do adore this blushing birdie, but if pink doesn't made you wink, you can switch out the candy melts for regular white chocolate and create an elegant swan. If you find your chocolate is a bit thick or at the early stages of seizing, quickly stir in a drop or two of cooking oil (any type will do) to loosen it up again.

INGREDIENTS

105G WHITE SUGAR PASTE

100G PINK CANDY MELTS

5G BLACK SUGAR PASTE

GOLD FOOD COLOURING

A LITTLE ICING SUGAR, FOR DUSTING

METHOD

1. Cut out a large sheet of greaseproof paper and trace the flamingo from the template chapter.
2. Tip the candy melts into a heatproof bowl. Melt the chocolate in short bursts in the microwave, stirring every 20 seconds. Ideally, you want to melt the chocolate gradually rather than just nuking it. Short bursts and quick stirs are the best way to go about this.
3. Drop two tablespoons of chocolate onto the flamingo template, gently spreading until it meets the edges.
4. Use a teaspoon to drop dollops of chocolate onto the paper. Using a pastry brush or spoon, spread the chocolate into feathers. Leave to set for 30 mins, or until firm.
5. Dust the worktop with a little icing sugar. Roll out the white sugar paste and cut out a 20cm circle. Place it on top of your tart.
6. Dunk a paintbrush in gold food colouring and splatter across the surface of the tart.

7. Carefully peel the chocolate pieces from the paper. Place the flamingo neck piece on top of the icing before layering up the feathers. Roll out the black icing and use the template to cut out the beak and eyelashes. Use the white icing offcuts to create the stripe and the crown.
8. Stick the icing pieces to the tart using a paintbrush dipped in water. Paint the crown with the gold food colouring to finish.

Quick and Easy Decoration Ideas

I get it, sometimes time and patience are not on our side. You need a beautiful dessert, but the kids are fighting, it's pouring down outside and the dog just hot-footed it out of the kitchen with your rolling pin. Here's my list of quick and easy decorations that are stress-free and darn delicious to boot. Zero artistic flair required.

CARAMELISED NUTS

Toast pecans, walnuts or almonds in a dry pan for 3–5 mins. In a separate small pan, melt 50g caster sugar until golden. Stir in the nuts, coating evenly. Scatter over cream-filled tarts and drizzle any remaining caramel in thin streams. Let cool before serving.

FRUIT AND HERBS

Layer thinly sliced seasonal fruits (peach, plum, berries) in a loose spiral or concentric circle. Tuck tiny mint leaves, thyme sprigs or edible flowers between the slices. The herbs will add aroma and visual interest without overpowering the fruit, adding an expensive-looking addition with very little effort.

CHOCOLATE SHARDS

Use a vegetable peeler or knife to create chocolate shards. Stick a few upright into mousse or cream, scatter some flat. Dust lightly with cocoa or edible gold for subtle sparkle. It's certainly worth popping the chocolate in the freezer for 30 mins beforehand if you have particularly warm hands.

MARBLED SWIRLS

For dual-flavour fillings (e.g., raspberry and vanilla), drop large dollops of each filling on top of the tart and swirl lightly with a skewer. Imperfect, organic patterns are best.

NUT BUTTER DRIZZLE

Warm 2–3 tbsp of almond, hazelnut or peanut butter until pourable. Drizzle over tarts in thin arcs. Finish with a sprinkling of chopped toasted nuts for extra texture.

FREEZE-DRIED FRUIT

Lightly crush freeze-dried raspberries, strawberries or mango. Scatter over the tart, letting some pieces sink slightly into the cream for depth. Alternatively, drizzle melted dark chocolate over the tart and sprinkle with freeze-dried berries before setting.

EDIBLE FLOWER PETAL CONFETTI

Scatter edible petals (pansies, nasturtiums, rose petals) unevenly across cream or custard tarts. Dust lightly with icing sugar for a fresh, ethereal effect. Many supermarkets sell jars of dried, crushed rose petals in the herbs and spices section, which work just as well as fresh.

MINI MERINGUE KISSES

Pipe or spoon tiny meringue kisses on top of your tart in loose clusters. Lightly torch the tips for colour. A delicious addition for cream or fruit tarts.

SPICED SUGAR AND ZEST

Mix 1 tsp caster sugar with a pinch of cinnamon or nutmeg. Finely grate citrus zest over the top and lightly sprinkle the spiced sugar. This works particularly well on pumpkin, custard or cream tarts for a fresh, yet autumnal, twist.

TEXTURED DRIZZLE AND CRUMBS

Combine a thin chocolate or caramel drizzle with chopped nuts, crushed cookies, or biscuit crumbs. Let the drips run naturally over the edges for additional rustic charm.

CRISPY CARAMEL LACE

Melt 50g sugar until golden and drizzle in a lacy pattern on parchment (the faster you shake your implement, the finer and more intricate the caramel decoration will be). Leave to cool before placing it on top of the tart. Sprinkle a little sea salt over the top for flavour and contrast.

SEASONAL BERRY STACK

Cluster blueberries, currants or gooseberries at the centre, letting some spill over naturally. Perfect for a freshly gathered, summer garden look. Finish with a flourish of sifted icing sugar.

CANDIED CITRUS RIBBONS

Peel citrus into thin ribbons. Heat 50g caster sugar with 2 tbsp water to create a syrup. Blanch the citrus pieces in the syrup for 3 mins. Leave to cool slightly, twist and scatter over the tarts. Great with lemon, cream or custard fillings.

AUTUMN SPICE BLEND

Sift a mixture of cinnamon, nutmeg and ginger over the tarts using a fine sieve (preferably over a stencil, if you have any to hand). This comforting blend creates a warm aroma and subtle colour for autumn/winter tarts.

CHOCOLATE CURLS

Wrap a sheet of greaseproof paper around a jar or food tin. Melt some chocolate in a double boiler and leave to cool slightly. Spoon the chocolate over the paper in quick flicks of the wrist. Leave to set completely before carefully removing from the paper and transferring to the tart.

CANDIED NUT CLUSTER

Coat nuts (almond, hazelnut, whatever you fancy) in caster sugar and toast over a medium heat until golden. Cluster in small groups on top of your tart, crushing a few to scatter for texture.

EDIBLE GLITTER HERBS

Dust edible glitter lightly over herbs such as mint, thyme and rosemary for a wintery, frosty morning effect.

TOASTED COCONUT FLAKES

Lightly toast some coconut flakes in a dry pan, giving it a shake every 30 seconds to avoid burning. Scatter over cream or tropical tarts, pressing a few gently into the filling for texture.

HONEYCOMB CHUNKS

Break honeycomb into uneven pieces. Arrange on chocolate or caramel tarts, letting some stick out at angles for height. If you want to make your own, heat 100g caster sugar with 3 tbsp golden syrup until fully melted. Add 1 tsp bicarbonate of soda and whisk quickly as it foams. Pour the mixture onto a large sheet of greaseproof paper and leave to set for 30 mins.

MARBLED WHITE AND DARK CHOCOLATE

Drop blobs of melted white and dark chocolate onto a well-chilled tart. Swirl lightly with a skewer and leave to set. Imperfect swirls give a patisserie look, so don’t get too hung up on making it look a certain way.

PEAR AND ALMOND FAN

Thinly slice pears and brush with lemon juice to prevent browning. Arrange them in a fan from the centre of the tart and sprinkle with chopped, toasted almonds. The perfect pairing for frangipane and custard tarts.

FREEZE-DRIED FRUIT DUST

Grind freeze-dried fruit to a fine powder. Dust lightly over cream or custard tarts for colour and subtle tartness. Have a play around with stencils if you have any to hand.

CINNAMON STICK AND STAR ANISE ACCENTS

Place a small stack of cinnamon stick and star anise at a gentle angle on the top of autumn/winter tarts. Dust lightly with icing sugar or cocoa and remember to remove before eating.

THIN APPLE OR PEACH SLICES

Slice fruit paper-thin (a mandoline is perfect for precise slices) and arrange in concentric circles or overlapping layers. Brush with gently heated apricot jam for extra shimmer and shine.

MINI MACARONS

Decorate your tart with store-bought mini macarons. I find mixing them with edible flowers and arranging them in a crescent shape creates a beautifully chic effect.

CHOCOLATE-DIPPED FRUIT

Dip berries or citrus segments in chocolate and refrigerate until set. Rest at an angle in the centre of the tart.

SPICED CRUMB LAYER

Mix crushed biscuits with a pinch of cinnamon or nutmeg and 1–2 tbsp of melted butter. Sprinkle over cream or custard tarts for a toasty, crumble-like finish.

PIPED CREAM ROSETTES

Use a small star nozzle to pipe whipped cream rosettes along the edge. Alternate with small fruits, nuts or chocolate curls.

CHOCOLATE LATTICE

Pipe melted chocolate in a loose lattice over chilled tarts. Let some lines drip over the edge for casual elegance. Finish with fresh fruit and herbs.

CANDIED GINGER PIECES

Dice candied ginger and scatter lightly over the top of the tart. For extra indulgence, dip the ginger in melted dark chocolate and leave to set before using.

CARAMEL DRIP EDGE

A cheeky little cheat: slowly spoon store-bought tinned caramel along the tart edges, letting it drip naturally down the sides. Leave to set before serving.

MINI CHOCOLATE DECORATIONS

Melt 50g chocolate in a double boiler and pour into discs, swirls and flourishes on a sheet of greaseproof paper. Chill until set before placing upright on your tart for height and playful texture.

FRUIT COMPOTE DABS

Spoon thick fruit compote (raspberry, cherry, fig) in small blobs over cream tarts. This looks particularly lovely peeking out from beneath fresh fruit or edible flowers.

LAYERED *GELÉE* CUBES

Heat 100g fruit compote and 30g caster sugar until dissolved. Soften a sheet of gelatine in cold water, squeezing out any excess liquid before whisking it into the fruit mixture. Pour the mixture into a rectangular tray and chill until firm. Cut into tiny cubes and scatter over cream or custard tarts for a modern, geometric look.

WHIPPED CREAM WAVES

Use a palette knife to create soft waves of whipped cream. Dust lightly with cocoa, cinnamon or zest for subtle colour and texture. If you're struggling with the palette knife, spoon a teaspoon of cream onto the tart, using the back of the spoon to swoosh it away. Repeat until your design is complete.

Special Projects: Minis, Celebrations and More

EASY

Festive Mincemeat Tart

85 MINS

Oh, I do love a generous slice of this festive tart topped with a boulder of vanilla ice cream. If you have no Christmassy cutters to hand, you can omit the decorative parts and bake as a regular tart. Delicious nonetheless.

INGREDIENTS

340G MINCEMEAT

275G PLAIN FLOUR

50G GOLDEN CASTER SUGAR

75G UNSALTED BUTTER, CHILLED AND CUBED

55G VEGETABLE SHORTENING (SUCH AS TREX)

1 LARGE EGG

30ML BRANDY

30ML COLD WATER

1 TBSP ROYAL ICING

SUGAR PEARLS

ICING SUGAR, FOR DUSTING

METHOD

1. Stir the flour and caster sugar together. Add the unsalted butter and vegetable shortening, rubbing the fat into the dry ingredients with your fingertips.
2. Stir in the brandy, water and egg, bringing the dough together.
3. Wrap the dough in cling film and chill for 30 mins.
4. Preheat the oven to 200°/180° (fan)/gas mark 6.
5. Roll the pastry out onto a lightly floured surface. Use it to line your 20cm tart tin.
6. Place a sheet of baking paper over the pastry and fill with baking beans or uncooked rice. Bake for 15 mins.
7. Remove the paper and filling from the tin. Bake for a further 5 mins.

8. Add the mincemeat and return the tart to the oven for 10 mins. Meanwhile, roll out the remaining pastry and cut out an assortment of Christmas shapes such as gingerbread men and stars. Bake in the oven for 7 mins.
9. Leave the tart and decorations to cool completely. Add the decorations to the crust, using a little royal icing when needed. Add some sugar pearls and a dusting of icing sugar.

Morello Cherry and Almond Tart

EASY

90 MINS

An easy tart for a lazy day, this dairy-free option contains zero butter in the pastry, resulting in a super-flaky crumb. Feel free to add a couple of daisies for a whimsical, 'picnic on a summer's day' vibe.

INGREDIENTS

240G PLAIN FLOUR

125G VEGETABLE SHORTENING (SUCH AS TREX)

90–100ML ICED WATER

PINCH OF SALT

FOR THE FILLING

580G CHERRIES

225G CASTER SUGAR

2 TBSP CORNFLOUR

1 TSP ALMOND EXTRACT

PINCH OF SALT

METHOD

1. Remove the stones from the cherries (you can buy a special tool for this, which will save heaps of time). Toss them in a pan with the sugar, cornflour, almond extract and salt. Leave to stand for 30 mins.
2. Place the pan on a medium heat and bring to a boil. Allow the mixture to thicken before leaving to cool overnight.
3. Make the pastry by rubbing together the flour, vegetable shortening and salt. Add the water, a little at a time, until the pastry comes together. Wrap in cling film and refrigerate for 30 mins.
4. Roll the pastry out onto a lightly floured worktop. Use it to line your tart tin, leaving a slight overhang.

5. Use decorative cutters to cut out some pastry shapes for the top of the tart.
6. Preheat the oven to 190°/170° (fan)/gas mark 5.
7. Transfer the cherry filling to the tart case and bake for 45 mins.
8. Sprinkle a little sugar over the decorative pieces and bake for approximately 10 mins or until golden.
9. Remove the tart from the oven and arrange the decorative pieces across the top. Garnish with some edible flowers if you like, and serve with a generous slosh of custard.

EASY

Pistachio and Praline Chocolate Bar

80 MINS

INGREDIENTS

200G PLAIN FLOUR

60G ICING SUGAR

30G COCOA POWDER

100G UNSALTED BUTTER, CHILLED AND CUBED

2 EGG YOLKS

A LITTLE ICED WATER

FOR THE PRALINE

75G PISTACHIOS

80G CASTER SUGAR

150ML DOUBLE CREAM

200G DARK CHOCOLATE, CHOPPED

30ML WATER

FOR THE GANACHE

160ML DOUBLE CREAM

40ML MILK

200G DARK CHOCOLATE, CHOPPED

TO DECORATE

CHOPPED PISTACHIOS

EDIBLE FLOWERS

BERRIES

METHOD

1. Start by making the pastry. Sieve together the flour, icing sugar and cocoa. Rub in the butter using the tips of your fingers, until the mixture resembles fine breadcrumbs.
2. Stir in the egg yolks and add the iced water a spoonful at a time until the dough comes together. Wrap the dough in cling film and refrigerate for 30 mins.
3. For the praline, gently heat the caster sugar and water until an amber caramel has formed (do not stir, however tempted you may be to do so). Spread the pistachios onto a sheet of baking paper and pour the caramel over the top. Leave to cool completely before snapping into shards and blitzing in a food processor.

4. Heat the 150ml double cream until it reaches scalding point. Stir in the 200g chopped chocolate and blitzed praline. Set aside.
5. Preheat the oven to 180°/160° (fan)/gas mark 4. Roll out the pastry onto a lightly floured surface and use it to line a 36cm oblong tart tin (a large round tin will also do). Prick the base several times with a fork and pop it back in the fridge for a further half hour.
6. Line the pastry base with paper and baking beans. Bake for 10 mins before removing the beans and liner. Bake for a further 10 mins before leaving to cool completely.
7. Scoop the praline into the pastry case, smoothing it out evenly.
8. Make the ganache topping by heating the remaining cream and milk until the edges start to bubble. Remove the pan from the heat and stir in the chopped dark chocolate. Immediately pour the ganache over the praline and leave to set.
9. Decorate your tart with chopped pistachios, edible flowers or fruit. Keep refrigerated and serve with a dollop of ice cream.

EASY

Cheat's Raspberry and Mascarpone Cream Tarts

20 MINS

These cheeky little numbers *just* about qualify as tarts but are an excellent dessert or elevenses treat when time is short, and supplies are low. Any berries will do for the topping; go with whatever you have lurking in the fridge.

INGREDIENTS

85G MASCARPONE

20G CASTER SUGAR

1 TSP LEMON JUICE

1 TSP LEMON ZEST

1 TSP VANILLA EXTRACT

1 SHEET PUFF PASTRY (STORE-BOUGHT)

1 EGG, BEATEN

15G CASTER SUGAR

250G RASPBERRIES

SPRIG OF MINT

ICING SUGAR, TO FINISH

METHOD

1. Preheat the oven to 200°/180° (fan)/gas mark 6.
2. Unroll the puff pastry. Use a cookie cutter or a mug to cut out eight pastry circles. Use a smaller cutter or beaker to emboss a circle in the centre of each disc.
3. Whisk together the mascarpone, caster sugar, lemon juice, zest and vanilla extract. Divide the mixture between the pastry discs and smooth out with the back of a spoon.
4. Top the pastry discs with raspberries. Brush the edges of the pastry with a little beaten egg and sprinkle with caster sugar.
5. Bake in the oven for 15–18 mins before leaving to cool on a wire rack. Garnish with mint leaves and dust with icing sugar before serving.

EASY

Valentine's galette

90 mins

A galette is a free-form, flat tart that does not require a fluted tin. A baking sheet lined with baking paper will work just fine. I've shaped this into a heart for a pretty Valentine's treat, but you can stick to a simple circle, a rectangle, whatever you like.

INGREDIENTS

90G PLAIN FLOUR

50G CASTER SUGAR

PINCH OF SALT

120G COLD, UNSALTED BUTTER, CUBED

60ML ICED WATER

1 SMALL EGG, BEATEN

1 TBSP SOFT BROWN SUGAR

FOR THE FILLING

400G STRAWBERRIES, HULLED

50G CASTER SUGAR

1 TBSP VANILLA EXTRACT

TO SERVE

2 STEMS FRESH MINT LEAVES

VANILLA ICE CREAM

METHOD

1. Slice the strawberries and pop them in a bowl with the caster sugar and vanilla. Give the bowl a shake and leave to macerate for 15 mins.
2. If making your own pastry, rub the flour and butter together until the mixture resembles fine breadcrumbs. Add the salt and caster sugar. Stir in the water little by little until a dough comes together. Wrap in clingfilm and refrigerate for 15 mins.
3. Preheat the oven to 200°/180° (fan)/gas mark 6. Line a tray with baking paper.
4. Roll out your chilled/pre bought pastry. Use a sharp knife to trim away some of the edges to create a large heart shape. Top with the strawberries, leaving a gap of 2cm around the edge.

5. Brush the exposed edge with a little beaten egg. Fold the edges in on themselves, allowing the pastry to pleat as you go.
6. If you have a cutter at home, cut some heart-shaped pieces out of the leftover pastry. Use a little egg to stick the hearts to the pleated edges before brushing the entire frame with egg.
7. Sprinkle the pastry with brown sugar and bake for 25–30 mins. Leave to cool on a wire rack.
8. When the galette has cooled, drizzle with the residual juices from the macerated strawberries. Decorate with mint leaves and serve with a generous scoop of vanilla ice cream.

EASY

Passionfruit Celebration Bar

1 HOUR

A lovely alternative to a birthday cake. Slice into slim bars and serve with a shot of coconut rum (age permitting, of course). The rectangular shape is perfect for piped messages and jolly greetings, just keep the fruit additions to the edges of the tart and add your text to the middle.

INGREDIENTS

250G DIGESTIVE BISCUITS
150G UNSALTED BUTTER
250G CREAM CHEESE
120G PASSIONFRUIT CURD
120G WHITE CHOCOLATE SPREAD
120ML DOUBLE CREAM

TO DECORATE

100ML DOUBLE CREAM
2 TBSP ICING SUGAR
2 TBSP PASSIONFRUIT CURD
50G STRAWBERRIES
50G RASPBERRIES
MINT LEAVES

METHOD

1. Crush the biscuits into crumbs, making sure no clumps remain. Melt the butter and stir it into the crumb mixture.
2. Transfer to a 36cm oblong loose-based tart tin. Use the back of a spoon to compress the mixture into the base and ridges.
3. Beat together the cream cheese, passionfruit curd and white chocolate spread. Set aside.
4. Whip the cream until thick, glossy peaks form. Fold one third of the cream into the curd mixture, being mindful not to overbeat. Gentle folding motions with the spatula are all you need. Repeat with the remaining cream.

5. Spoon the filling into the tart case and smooth over with a palette knife. Dot the passionfruit curd over the surface before running a toothpick to and fro to create a marbled effect.
6. To decorate, whip the double cream and icing sugar until thick. Transfer to a piping bag fitted with a star nozzle.
7. Pipe stars of cream in an ad hoc fashion around the edges of the tart. Garnish with mint leaves and add the sliced fruit. Finish with a light dusting of icing sugar and keep refrigerated until serving.

EASY

Amaretto Bakewell Tartlets

40 MINS

INGREDIENTS

150G PLAIN FLOUR

75G COLD UNSALTED BUTTER, DICED

25G ICING SUGAR

1 MEDIUM EGG YOLK

1-2 TBSP COLD WATER

FOR THE FILLING

75G UNSALTED BUTTER, SOFTENED

75G CASTER SUGAR

1 MEDIUM EGG

75G GROUND ALMONDS

1 TBSP PLAIN FLOUR

1 TBSP AMARETTO LIQUEUR

6 TSP CHERRY JAM

FOR THE ICING

150G ICING SUGAR

2-3 TBSP WATER OR MORE AMARETTO

6 TSP CHERRY JAM

EDIBLE FLOWERS

METHOD

1. Preheat the oven to 160°/140° (fan)/gas mark 3. Grease a six-hole tart tin and add a sprinkling of icing sugar.
2. Make the pastry by rubbing together the flour and butter until the mixture resembles coarse breadcrumbs. Mix in icing sugar before adding the yolk and water to form dough. Wrap in cling film and chill for 30 mins.
3. Roll pastry out on a lightly floured worktop to about 3mm thick. Use a large cookie cutter to cut out six circles to line the tart tins. Refrigerate for 10 mins.

4. Line the pastry cases with baking parchment and baking beans or uncooked rice. Bake for 10 mins. Remove paper and beans and bake for 5 mins more.
5. Make the frangipane by beating the butter and sugar until fluffy, then beating in the egg. Stir in the almonds, flour and amaretto.
6. Spoon 1 tsp cherry jam into each case and top with a generous teaspoon of frangipane. Bake for 20–25 mins until golden and set. Leave to cool on a wire rack before turning the tarts out of their tins.
7. Mix the icing sugar with water or amaretto to create a thick but pourable icing. Spread over each tart before adding a dollop of cherry jam and swirling with a toothpick.
8. Top each tart with an edible flower or two, and leave to set completely.

EASY

Strawberry Lemonade Scone Tart

45 MINS

If you leave English soil for more than five days, you are required by law to have tea and scones within 24 hours of re-entry or face up to 10 years jail time. Best play it safe with this scone/tart hybrid infused with lemonade for a fluffy, lightly scented crumb.

INGREDIENTS

375G SELF-RAISING FLOUR

250ML DOUBLE CREAM

250ML LEMONADE (FULL SUGAR)

FOR THE TOPPING

100G STRAWBERRY JAM

250ML DOUBLE CREAM

200G STRAWBERRIES, HULLED AND SLICED

EDIBLE FLOWERS, TO DECORATE

METHOD

1. Preheat the oven to 180°/160° (fan)/gas mark 4. Lightly grease your 20cm fluted tart tin.
2. Sift the flour into a large bowl. Add the cream and lemonade, stirring vigorously until well mixed.
3. Transfer the scone mixture into the tart tin and bake for 30–35 mins. Leave the scone in its tin as it cools.
4. When the scone is completely cold, level off the top with a knife. Spread the jam in an even layer over the base.
5. Whip the cream until thick and glossy. Dollop it over the jam before topping with the sliced strawberries and edible flowers. Keep refrigerated until serving.

ADVANCED

Summer Solstice Showstopper

2 HOURS

A stunning tart for the longest day of the year (although you can, of course, enjoy it any time you like). This tart requires a little more time and patience, thanks to the meringues, but you can always make them in advance and store them in an airtight container.

INGREDIENTS

200G PLAIN FLOUR

100G UNSALTED BUTTER, CHILLED AND CUBED

50G ICING SUGAR

PINCH OF SALT

1 MEDIUM EGG YOLK

2–3 TBSP ICED WATER

FOR THE FILLING

250G MASCARPONE CHEESE

60G ICING SUGAR

200ML DOUBLE CREAM

1 TSP VANILLA EXTRACT

FOR THE MERINGUE KISSES

2 LARGE EGG WHITES

100G CASTER SUGAR

GEL FOOD COLOURING IN PINK, ORANGE AND YELLOW

TO DECORATE

EDIBLE FLOWERS AND MINT LEAVES

METHOD

1. Make the pastry by rubbing together the flour, butter and salt with your fingertips. The mixture should look like fine breadcrumbs with no clumps.
2. Stir in the icing sugar. Add the egg yolk and 2 tbsp of chilled water, mixing gently until a dough forms. If it's looking a little dry, add an extra tablespoon of water.
3. Shape the dough into a disc before wrapping in cling film and refrigerating for 30 mins.
4. Preheat the oven to 180°/160° (fan)/gas mark 4.

5. Roll out the pastry on a lightly floured surface. Gently transfer it to a 20cm tart tin and trim the edges.
6. Line the tart case with baking paper and fill with baking beans or uncooked rice. Bake for 15 mins.
7. Remove the beans and the paper, then bake for a further 10 mins until golden. Leave to cool completely.
8. Make the filling by beating together the mascarpone, icing sugar and vanilla extract until smooth.
9. In a separate bowl, whip the cream to soft peaks. Fold the cream into the mascarpone mixture a third at a time, ensuring everything is well combined.
10. Spread the filling into the cooled tart shell. Chill while you prepare the meringues.
11. Decrease the oven temperature to 100°/80° (fan)/gas mark ¼. Line two baking trays with parchment.
12. Whisk the egg whites in a clean bowl until they form stiff peaks.
13. Add the caster sugar 1 tbsp at a time, whisking continuously between additions. Continue until the meringue is glossy and smooth (if you rub a tiny amount between your fingers you should not feel any sugar grains).
14. Divide the mixture into three bowls. Stir in a tiny dab of each food colour gel to create three shades.
15. Transfer the meringue mixtures into three piping bags fitted with large star nozzles. Pipe medium-sized kisses onto the trays.
16. Bake for 60–75 mins, until the meringues can be lifted cleanly from the parchment. Leave to cool completely.
17. Use a paintbrush to splatter some extra food colouring over the meringues. You can stick to like with like, or use contrasting colours for an eclectic effect.
18. Remove the tart from the fridge and arrange the coloured meringue kisses over the top, mixing sizes and colours for a playful look.
19. Finish with edible flowers and mint leaves. Enjoy.

Tropical Celebration Tart

EASY

1 hour

A tangy tart for all year round, this tropical cutie is one of my favourite showstoppers. The mango roses are easier to construct than you might think; you simply slice, roll, and secure them into the tart filling. Compliments incoming ...

INGREDIENTS

200G PLAIN FLOUR

100G UNSALTED BUTTER, COLD AND CUBED

75G ICING SUGAR

1 EGG YOLK

1–2 TBSP COCONUT RUM, CHILLED

FOR THE FILLING

200G COCONUT CREAM, CHILLED

200G MASCARPONE

75G ICING SUGAR

ZEST AND JUICE OF 1 LIME

1 TSP VANILLA EXTRACT

TO DECORATE

1 SMALL RIPE MANGO, PEELED AND FINELY SLICED

A HANDFUL OF WHITE STRAWBERRIES (OR REGULAR STRAWBERRIES IF UNAVAILABLE)

PULP OF TWO PASSIONFRUIT

FRESH PHYSALIS, HUSKS OPENED

METHOD

1. Rub the flour and butter together until the mix resembles fine breadcrumbs. Stir in the icing sugar.
2. Add the egg yolk and rum, bringing the dough together with a butter knife. If it seems a little dry, add a splash more rum.
3. Wrap the dough in cling film and chill for 30 mins.

4. Roll the pastry out on a lightly floured worktop and use it to line your 20cm tart tin. Prick the base with a fork and chill for 15 mins.
5. Preheat the oven to 180°/160° (fan)/gas mark 4.
6. Line the tart with baking paper and fill with baking beans or uncooked rice. Bake for 15 mins before removing the paper and beans. Bake for a further 8–10 mins until golden. Leave to cool.
7. Make the filling by whisking together the coconut cream and mascarpone until smooth.
8. Add the icing sugar, lime zest, lime juice and vanilla extract. Beat until thick and creamy.

9. Add the filling to the cooled crust. Create a swirl from the centre of the tart using the back of a spoon.
10. Arrange the mango slices into rose shapes by rolling them into spirals and placing evenly around the tart. If the sides feel a little floppy, bolster them with the other fruits.
11. Nestle the strawberries and physalis around the roses. Spoon the passionfruit pulp over the fruit.
12. Keep chilled until serving.

EASY

Lemon and Chocolate Tartlet Platter

90 MINS

Torn between indulgent and rich, and light and zesty? Great news: this split batch has both. Using the same crusts but different fillings, you can have double the flavour in the same amount of time as a single batch. Win-win.

INGREDIENTS

120G PLAIN FLOUR

60G GROUND ALMONDS (OR HAZELNUTS, IF YOU PREFER)

40G ICING SUGAR

90G UNSALTED BUTTER, COLD AND CUBED

1 EGG YOLK

1 TBSP COLD WATER

FOR THE GANACHE FILLING

100G DARK CHOCOLATE (AROUND 70%), CHOPPED

100ML DOUBLE CREAM

15G UNSALTED BUTTER

FOR THE LEMON FILLING

75G CASTER SUGAR

ZEST AND JUICE OF 2 LEMONS

60G UNSALTED BUTTER, CUBED

2 EGGS

FOR THE MERINGUE TOPPING

2 EGG WHITES

100G CASTER SUGAR

½ TSP CREAM OR TARTAR, OR A FEW DROPS OF LEMON JUICE

TO DECORATE

FRESH FRUIT, CITRUS ZEST, OR EDIBLE PEARLS

METHOD

1. In a large bowl, rub together the butter into the flour, ground nuts and icing sugar.
2. Stir in the egg yolk and bring the dough together, adding a splash of water if it feels a little dry. Wrap the dough in cling film and refrigerate for 30 mins.

3. Roll out the dough onto a lightly floured worktop. Cut out circles to fit your tartlet tins.
4. Press the dough circles into your tartlet tins and prick the bases before chilling for 15 mins.
5. Preheat the oven to 180°/160° (fan)/gas mark 5.
6. Bake the tartlet crusts for 15–18 mins, or until golden. Leave to cool.
7. Make the ganache by heating the cream until just steaming. Pour it over the chopped dark chocolate and butter. Leave to work its magic for 2 mins.
8. Gently stir the ganache until smooth and glossy. Spoon it into half of the cooled pastry cases and leave to set at room temperature.

9. Make the lemon filling by whisking together the eggs, sugar, lemon juice and zest in a heatproof bowl.
10. Place the bowl over a pan of gently simmering water, whisking constantly until thickened.
11. Remove the bowl from the heat and whisk in the butter until smooth and glossy.
12. Spoon the lemon filling into the remaining pastry cases and chill until set.
13. Make the meringue topping by whisking the egg whites until foamy. Gradually add the sugar, whisking until stiff, glossy peaks form. Fold in the cream of tartar or lemon juice.
14. Pipe or spoon the meringue onto the lemon tartlets, toasting with a culinary blowtorch until burnished and crisp.
15. Use any fruit, herbs or sprinkles you have to hand to add a final flourish to your tarts. Enjoy.

Vanilla Meadow Tarts

EASY

1 HOUR

These midsummer beauties are formed in 11 x 6cm rectangular tart tins for the perfect dessert portion. Dried daisies and fresh rosemary from the garden add an elegant flourish without any additional work. A lazy treat for hazy days.

INGREDIENTS

200G DIGESTIVE BISCUITS, CRUSHED

90G UNSALTED BUTTER, MELTED

1 TBSP CASTER SUGAR

FOR THE FILLING

250ML DOUBLE CREAM

150G WHITE CHOCOLATE, FINELY CHOPPED

1 TSP VANILLA BEAN PASTE (OR SEEDS SCRAPED FROM 1 VANILLA POD)

PINCH OF SALT

TO DECORATE

DRIED DAISIES AND FRESH ROSEMARY

METHOD

1. Crush the biscuits finely, either in a food processor or give them a good bash with a rolling pin.
2. Stir in the melted butter and sugar until the mixture resembles damp sand. Divide between the tart tins, pressing firmly into the base and up the sides. Use the back of a spoon to compact the biscuit and get an even finish. Pop the tins in the fridge for at least 30 mins or until set.
3. Heat 125ml of the cream in a small pan until the edges start to bubble.
4. Remove the pan from the heat and pour over the white chocolate. Leave it to melt for 2 mins.
5. Gently stir in the vanilla and salt. Leave to cool slightly.

6. Whip the remaining cream until it reaches soft peaks. Fold it into the cooled chocolate mixture until the colour is cohesive and no swirls remain.
7. Spoon the filling into the chilled tart bases and smooth over the tops. Add the daisies and rosemary before chilling for 1 hour.

Using the templates that follow is easy-blooming peasy. Trace over your chosen template using baking/greaseproof paper. Run a knife or tracing wheel over the outline, remove the paper and cut out with a sharp knife. Donezo.

Tip: You don't need to trace an individual template for each part of the design. Draw the design in its entirety and re-use it for each piece. The paper can take it as long as you're not too heavy-handed.

Templates

Note: Double the size

Retro Ink

Fox in the Flowers

Pup Tart

Note: Double the size

Chalkboard

Smooth Sailing

Up & Away

Teddy Time

Rainbow Road

Pinkie Pie

Goodnight, Moon

Queen Cottontail

Paris in Springtime

Playing Dress Up

Recommended Suppliers

- **Tart tins:** I have used the Tala Performance 20cm fluted flan dish for the majority of the tarts in this book. You can pick one up at www.talacooking.com, Amazon, or Dunelm. All other tins came from www.amazon.com.
- **Moulds:** The mould used for the winter village tart is from www.karendaviessugarcraft.co.uk. All other moulds are from www.amazon.com.
- **Chocolate:** For coloured chocolate decorations, I use PME Candy Buttons. For all other chocolate decorations I use Dr. Oetker couverture.
- **Rice paper:** I use Bamboo Tree Vietnamese rice paper circles (spring roll wraps), available in most large supermarkets.
- **Wafer paper:** Edible wafer paper/tissue by Squires Kitchen. The 5cm (2in) round paper punch was from www.hobbycraft.co.uk.
- **Colours:** Both the edible lustre dusts and gel food colourings are by Sugarflair and are available on multiple sites online.
- **Rejuvenator spirit:** I use Sugarflair rejuvenator, although vodka works just as well.
- **Icing:** 'The Sugarpaste' from www.thecakedecoratingcompany.co.uk is terrific. However, as tarts are flat, any generic brand sugar paste (also known as 'ready to roll icing') will do.
- **Tracing wheel:** I use haberdashery tracing wheels as they are sturdy and last a long time (I am still using my mum's one from the 1970s). You can pick one up online or at any fabric/haberdashery store.

Acknowledgements

Writing this book has been its own kind of journey, one filled with late nights, flour in my hair and more cups of tea than I can count. I couldn't have done it without the people who've stood behind me, lifted me up and kept me going when it all felt a bit too much.

To my family and friends: thank you for being my anchor. For the endless patience, encouragement and laughter that have carried me through every chapter of life, as well as this book.

To everyone who has ever bought a cake from Vanilla Nova or read my column over the last 15 years: you've been a part of my story in ways you may not even realise. Every order, every shared post showing what you've made, has shaped the baker I've become. You've given me the confidence to keep experimenting, creating and sharing.

To those who have made me tea, listened to me grumble, celebrated the wins and held me steady through the losses, thank you. You've been my comfort through rejections, my cheerleader in competitions and my safe space when life has felt heavy.

To those who have taken a chance on me: my editors and agents, past and present. I wouldn't still be doing this if it weren't for you,

To the friends (both real life and online) who have checked in when I've disappeared into the darker corners of my mind, your compassion has meant everything.

And finally, to you: the person holding this book. Thank you for inviting me into your kitchen, for giving these recipes a place in your life. I hope they bring you the same sense of peace and escape that baking has always given me. May these tarts be more than just food, may they be your quiet moment when the world gets a little too loud.

With love and gratitude,
Deb